# Encountering
# the Dark Goddess

A Journey into the Shadow Realms

# Encountering the Dark Goddess

## A Journey into the Shadow Realms

### Frances Billinghurst

**MOON
BOOKS**

Winchester, UK
Washington, USA

JOHN HUNT PUBLISHING

First published by Moon Books, 2021
Moon Books is an imprint of John Hunt Publishing Ltd., No. 3 East Street, Alresford
Hampshire SO24 9EE, UK
office@jhpbooks.net
www.johnhuntpublishing.com
www.moon-books.net

For distributor details and how to order please visit the 'Ordering' section on our website.

ISBN: 978 1 78904 599 4
978 1 78904 600 7 (ebook)
Library of Congress Control Number: 2020934412

A CIP catalogue record for this book is available from the British Library.

Design: Stuart Davies

UK: Printed and bound by CPI Group (UK) Ltd, Croydon, CR0 4YY
Printed in North America by CPI GPS partners

We operate a distinctive and ethical publishing philosophy in
all areas of our business, from our global network of authors to
production and worldwide distribution.

# Contents

To Mum and Dad, for your inspiration and support, both knowingly and unknowingly.

*To go in the dark with a light is to know the light.*
*To know the dark, go dark. Go without sight,*
*and find that the dark, too, blooms and sings,*
*and is travelled by dark feet and dark wings.*
(Wendell Berry[1])

A Gift in the Shadows
(Frances Billinghurst, 2016)

The night of endless darkness
I know you are there
With your ever silent embrace
A friend in the shadows.

When I am abandoned, neglected
Floundering in the ocean of uncertainty, despair
Blinded, groping for a sense of reason
I am alone, yet you are forever with me
Awaiting my complete surrender.

As I slide through all sense of clarity
Spinning in endless confusion
You remind me to inhale
To pause and wait.

From the deepest depths
The seed of light can be found
Illuminating the in-between spaces
Where the exquisite lotus emerges.

Persephone by Soror Basilisk

# Introduction

# Darkness and the Dark Goddess

Why does the word "dark" conjure up an element of fear in so many of us? Why do we continue to be afraid of the darkness once we have reached adulthood? Is it because of the unknown or unseen element that may have frightened us as a child lingers in our subconscious? Or is it simply the fact that it relates to the unexposed, the unfamiliar, or even the unrealised? Maybe it is because our Western society tends to associate "darkness" with "evil"? Or is it something else?

We seem to forget that in order to appreciate the light, we must come from a place of darkness. This darkness is not in the sense of "evil" or "foreboding", but of being a "void", an "emptiness". This emptiness is far from barren for it contains all the potential that may be brought into formation, into being. Just as the night's sky contains the stars, the Milky Way and all the other galaxies beyond our vision and knowledge, this can only truly be appreciated from a place of darkness.

All worldly creational myths begin with a period of darkness, a time before time, a sacred time before all life began. It is within this sacred darkness that the egg of light is first created and begins to grow. Darkness holds the peace which is reflected by the mother's womb from which we all are born, and the earth's tomb into which we eventually return. From darkness we are born and, in effect, into darkness we will all return. Does this mean therefore that we are in fact light shining within this darkness?

As indicated above, for Westerners, it is common for us to be, by and large, raised in a culture where even the words "black" or "dark" conjures up negativity. People who are perceived as not being able to control their "dark" urges are seen as "evil" or

1

"lacking morals". These dark urges often place people outside of what society considers to be wholesome and balanced. This is filled with contradictions as to who (or what) constitutes the governing body of this "society" and therefore overriding perceptions. Yet, we are encouraged to distrust anything that is dark, encased by shadows and not out in full view.

This perception of darkness as being associated with evil as opposed to light and goodness has its roots in the ancient Persian religion of Zoroastrianism that emerged around the middle of the 5th century BCE. Central to this monotheistic religion was an eternal creator of *asha* (all good things), Ahura Mazda, and any violations of this order gave rise to the uncreated *druj* (falsehood or deceit). It is this concept that the Christian concept, and therefore largely Western idealism, of good (God = light) verses evil (Satan = darkness) stems from, which often leads to confusion when dealing with the concept of darkness as a whole.

Within various Eastern cultures, however, the separation of "light" and "dark" is perceived as somewhat limiting. This is because the two aspects are needed in order to attain completeness. For example, within the Taoist belief there are two sides to the "perfect whole" – the *yin* (the dark side of the mountain) and the *yang* (the light side of the mountain). Neither aspect is separate from each other as they both contain a small opposing part within. Likewise, without the other aspect, neither is complete on its own.

To me, there are many positive and indeed important things that emerge from the darkness. It is within the dark recesses of Mother Earth that the seeds which become the crops that feed us germinate and commence their life span. Here, within nature, the concept of darkness is very much a necessary part of the whole. This is because life is endlessly cyclic in nature whereby living things must die, or be destroyed, in order to create room for change or growth. This concept is also reflected within each of us. We all hold a measure of both light and darkness. As such, we need to learn how to interact with our dark side so that the destructive forces therein do not control our behaviour. In the work I have been teaching for over 10 years, which forms the basis of this book, is where working with the darker aspects of the goddess, the divine feminine, can be most beneficial, especially on a deeper psychological level.

While darkness is naturally around us, it is becoming increasingly difficult to experience true darkness these days, especially amongst urban dwellers, and to truly experience the beauty that can be revealed, such as in the night's sky. Growing up in country New Zealand, I knew that every night I slept under the Milky Way, the Southern Cross and the other constellations. Moving to the city upon my journey into adulthood, and with the increasing amount of light pollution as we become more and more wired to 24 hour living, these natural wonders of the cosmos seem to be getting less easily recognisable and therefore less appreciated. Our modern cities never sleep, and the same can almost be said for us as we surround ourselves with an increasing number of light filling gadgets, ignoring and even preventing ourselves from experiencing true darkness. Modern research highlights the impact artificial light has on our being, not only psychologically, but also physically, mentally and emotionally.

As we constantly fill our lives with light, we lose the much-needed time and place for introspection and rest that darkness, especially night, can provide. Have you ever stopped and wondered what this modern light-filled lifestyle is doing to you on a deeper psychological level: this disassociation, disconnection and lack of appreciation of the darkness?

Another disturbing aspect of the darkness for some people is silence. This is because the quietness, the stillness, can be just as frightening as the darkness itself. True silence is becoming more and more difficult to experience. Even if we can find ourselves deep in the countryside or wilderness, far away from roads, power transformers, and other modern advantages, true silence may still not be obtained due to natural sounds around us. So much so that on the rare occasions when this level of silence can be attained, it appears to be deafening. An increasing number of people are finding they are not able to sleep without some kind of noise or external stimulus, occurring. Could it be they are potentially fearful of what maybe discovered within that quiet and therefore they do whatever they can to avoid the silence?

A number of years ago I was given a recording of renowned Buddhist teacher Sogyal Rinpoche reciting "Rest in Natural Great Peace", a poem by Nyoshul Khen Rinpoche. In this recording, the listener is encouraged to take some three minutes to relax their "exhausted mind that has been beaten helplessly by karma and neurotic thoughts, like the relentless fury of the pounding waves in the infinite ocean of samsara"[2]. At the conclusion of my meditation classes I like to share this recording with the attendees and over the years have noted, with a degree of interest, the response this short recording stirs in people. Mostly, it is one of peace and tranquillity, as Sogyal Rinpoche reminds us to still the mind "like a glass of muddy water", allowing the "mud" (our impurities) to sink to the bottom. However, some people demonstrate a degree of agitation as if the very thought of "resting" their mind becomes more of an issue than the recurrence of stress and anxiety which originally led them to seek out a meditation class to start with. Likewise, I have noticed a similar degree of agitation demonstrated by some attendees when asked to sit in silence. Could this agitation be a result of a direct result of being unfamiliar with experiencing silence?

It is when we sit in silence and when we sit in darkness (i.e., going within yourself), and allow it to embrace us that much wisdom and knowledge can be gained, as well as truth exposed. Is this what people are terrified of the most, at the deepest subconscious level – the realisation of one's true self? It is interesting food for thought.

## Identifying with the Dark Goddess

Before I go any further with this extensive introduction, and explain the concept of the "Dark Goddess", I feel it is best to briefly explain what, or probably more appropriately who, actually the goddess is, for not all readers may be familiar with this concept. For a more detailed explanation, I direct readers to my earlier book, *In Her Sacred Name: Writings on the Divine Feminine*[3], which provides information about the goddess together with additional resources for further exploration.

The concept of there being a divine feminine who was worshipped and revered in ancient times is clearly evidenced by archaeological discoveries that date back to the Palaeolithic[4] (Stone Age) era where the first representatives of humankind's spiritual (or even religious) observances have been discovered. These images were of the female form, leading to the belief that in the beginning of human spiritual belief, deity was perceived as female[5] - after all, it was the female of most species who "created" the new, who gave birth, and any part the male played seemed somewhat insignificant or forgotten about after the initial sexual encounter. This also suggested it was the feminine energy, which originally was perceived as being predominant, which gave rise to the great matriarchal (or probably more accurately, matrifocal[6]) cultures of ancient Sumer, Babylon and Crete, where the remnants of the goddess can still be found today.

Earliest figurines of the divine feminine found through Europe date back to the Upper Palaeolithic[7] period (35,000 to 10,000 BCE) and have been referred to as "Venus" figures, largely because they appeared with large pendulous breasts, and ample hips and thighs that seemed to indicate a connection with fertility. The "Venus of Willendorf", named after a site in Austria where this figurine was found, is probably one of the better-known representations of the ancient goddess. Made of limestone, this palm sized figurine (about 11 cm high) appeared to be some kind of fertility goddess with her large pendulous breasts (upon which a pair of slim arms rest), expanded stomach and thick thighs.

From these early beginnings, down to our present day, the concept of the divine feminine, the goddess, has never truly been forgotten. Within Hinduism, in particular, there are an abundance of goddesses (often referred to as devis which are synonymous with Shakti, the female aspect of the divine). The chief deity of the Japanese Shinto religion is the sun goddess, Amaterasu Omi Kami. While not often mentioned, the cult of the ancient Goddess can be found even in Christianity through Sophia (wisdom) and Hagia Sophia (holy wisdom) perceived as an expression of understanding the Holy Spirit within Orthodox and Roman Catholic Christianity, not to mention the Virgin Mary herself who, through her aspect as Our Lady of Guadalupe, is worshipped openly throughout Central and South America.

When it comes to the "Dark" Goddess, I am referring to the nature of the goddess as opposed to the colour of her skin. This concept of what is meant by "dark" can be perceived in several different ways. My own interpretation, and therefore that which is expressed throughout this book, draws inspiration from the Jungian psychological term of the "shadow", as in the need to "embrace one's own shadow". This aspect of the self within Jungian psychology refers to the hidden and often rejected (although not necessarily "evil") aspects of our own personality or consciousness which we choose not to acknowledge or to identify with.

As a psychoanalyst, Carl Jung worked with the concept of archetypes, which he based upon reoccurring figures in mythology: the mother, child, trickster, warrior, etc. From this perception, the Dark Goddess can be likened to a gatekeeper or guardian of the inner "hell" we all must descend into in order to address, accept and even reclaim the rejected aspects of our self (our own internal demons). While I am not a psychoanalyst or psychologist, I have been interested in Jung's concepts for over

25 years, as they align with my other interests of mythology and metaphysics. To me, the "Shadow Self" presents repressed memories stored within our unconscious which prevent us from reaching our fullest potential. I believe there is so much more to the Dark Goddess than utilising her as some kind of archetype residing over her realm of "hell". To me, she is very real and how we perceive the realms wherein she resides depend largely on our own perceptions of things, our own place of mind. From my own personal experience with the Dark Goddess, not only is she is the gatekeeper or guardian to aspects of rejection or that which is suppressed, but she is also a guide (or psychopomp) to an inner realm that enlightens and transforms the soul. There are many aspects to her, which may explain the placement of some goddesses who have found their way into this book. I expand upon this further in the next section.

The above indicates to me that there is a difference between Jung's archetypes and deity, even if the insights received when such work is undertaken can be very similar. When something is an archetype, this tends to indicate that this is a "universally understood symbol, or pattern of behaviour, a prototype upon which others are copied, patterned, or emulated"[8]. While the archetypes used within Jungian psychology are groupings found within the myths and cultural stories, there is a tendency to apply this thought to deity as well. A generalization, for example, is that the Dark Goddess is the only aspect of the goddess to use when undertaking "shadow work", and this is something that should be approached with a combination of caution and fear. Whilst I do not disagree that the darker aspects of the goddess can certainly assist in understanding "shadow" workings, I find it somewhat perturbing that deity is pigeonholed so easily based on what can only be human-orientated emotive perceptions.

Before we start labelling deity as being "dark" or "light", we should question what these two words mean to us and why we feel the need to separate them. Deity, to me, is simply that

- deity, the divine. How "light" or "dark" they are perceived is merely a reflection of our human mindset. In other words, deity can be likened to being an embodiment of nature – it simply "is" - just as an erupting volcano whose lava flow threatens villages and livelihoods can hardly be classified as "dark", or a lioness hunting down a wildebeest to feed her cubs. These things happen simply because they happen.

With that in mind, these particular "dark" aspects of the goddess are so-called because they more readily challenge us when we get too complacent in accepting things instead of taking steps to make necessary changes needed at a deeper soul level, as opposed to other aspects of the divine feminine which tend to influence us in more subtle ways. We find the Dark Goddess appearing in our lives when we least expect her. Sometimes it is within the silence that she will make herself known to us, like a shy child peeping around the corner, attempting to attract our attention. Often, she barges in with no regard to what we are doing or have planned, and simply takes over, causing chaos and havoc. She takes hold of our complacent lifestyle and shakes it like an angry cleaner attempting to remove dust from a floor covering. And there is nothing we can do about it.

Depending on what the concept of "darkness" means to you, some of the goddesses contained in the following pages may seem out of place as being classified as "dark". However, I perceive the Dark Goddess as spanning a number of different categories. She appears as the original creatrix of all things who was known as Tiamat to the Babylonians, the Cailleach to the inhabitants of the British Isles, and Nut[9] to the ancient Egyptians. She also has a destroying aspect where her goal is to free us from limitations and restrictions, with the Hindu Goddess Kali and the African Orisha, Oya, falling into this aspect. There are the "untamed ones", the Dark Goddesses who encourages us to operate on our own accord, often persuaded by our emotions. The Egyptian Sekhmet and her Hawaiian counterpart Pele fall into this category as they are both renowned for their anger, with the Hebraic Lilith challenging God with respect to her sexuality and role in relationships. The Dark Goddess also reminds us of our own mortality in one of the oldest known Hindu tantric goddesses Chumunda who is depicted having a skeleton body with blood on her teeth, wielding a bloody scythe and holding a severed head.

There are the Dark Goddesses who are rulers of the Underworld, and it is into their realm that we must enter in order to assess their knowledge. Before we do this, we need to acknowledge them in their own right. The Sumerian Ereshkigal is one such goddess, who tends to be more commonly referred to through the reciting of the descent of her sister Inanna, the Queen of Heaven, but who rarely seems to be explored in any great detail herself. The Greek Persephone, who, as the maiden Kore, was allegedly snatched from the upper world by Hades, whose own name is a reference to the Underworld, "a dark, cold mysterious place" according to the *Cambridge Dictionary*. This seems hardly a place a young maiden would desire to reside in, but she did and was transformed. It is this knowledge and wisdom of transformation that Persephone offers us in the form of her sacred pomegranate. The Egyptian Nephthys is often depicted as a shadowy reflection of her better-known sister, Isis, by modern writers, yet through her interesting past, she continues to hold the keys to discoveries of a deeper level – one of these being the wisdom obtained through the gift of silence. Then we have the initiators whose primary roles are to transform our lives (whether we are prepared for such a change or not): the Slavic Baba Yaga is able to arm us with the light of illumination should we be able to pass her tests, as well as the aforementioned Sumerian Ereshkigal who is involved in the transformation process as we ascend (like Inanna) from her Underworld.

As one of the main aspects of the Dark Goddess is to challenge us, it is not uncommon for her to shape shift and morph into any of the above categories, as well as others not already considered, appearing to us in whatever guise she decides on. The pre-Olympian Hekate demonstrates her ability to do just this by the way she has been depicted throughout history, if the number of differing epithets she was known by is anything to go by. As a result we are forced into being flexible when working with her, for it is in her very nature to challenge concepts, encouraging us to think outside the box (so to speak). This has confused modern writers who have aligned her Underworldly existence and connection with the dark phase of the moon with that of the older crone goddess. Yet, historically, Hekate seems to have been depicted only as a youthful maiden goddess.

Any categories mentioned above are listed extremely loosely, for the Dark Goddess does not take too kindly to being pigeonholed. The more you study the sacred myths, the more you will discover that there are many other goddesses who display elements of darkness, even on a temporary level through expressing qualities that we can all identify with. The Greek goddess Demeter, for example, entered into her own version of darkness when she lost her daughter and neglected her duties through her deep mourning. Within the Arthurian legend, Arthur's half-sister, Morgan le Fay, experiences a number of personal crises as she struggles to come to terms with her pre-destined role as High Priestess of Avalon. And who has not fallen foul of the Greek goddess of love Aphrodite and had their heart broken? This pigeonholing I explain in more detail in the next chapter, "Who is the Dark Goddess?"

Amongst the pages of this book a total of 13 goddesses can be found, all of whom fall under the realm "Dark Goddess", coming from ancient cultures where the concept of darkness and death were perceived as a natural part of existence. The number 13 is not a number selected randomly. As mentioned in my previous book[10], the moon enters its dark phase (when it appears to be hidden from earth) 13 times each year. This phase of the moon often relates to the "hidden" aspect of knowledge in many esoteric and metaphysical circles. Therefore, the original idea was that this book could be used to chart a year's journey of deep discovery, whereby each time, when the moon enters its dark phase, this marks the time when a journey with a new goddess can commence. Of course, after running workshops of the same name for over ten years, many more goddesses could have easily been included. However, I had to draw the line somewhere. I leave it up to the reader to choose. After reading the stories of these 13 goddesses there may be some who call to you and others who do not. I usually find it interesting to explore what you repel as there is often some personal connection (reflection of your soul self) on a deeper level.

So, this book is divided into three sections. The first section talks about the concept of the Dark Goddess as a whole, as well as the Jungian concept of the Shadow Self. The second section contains essays that outline interpretations of the sacred myths, poetry and other associations of the goddesses I have chosen to include an associated meditation you may wish to incorporate in order to commence establishing a relationship with them. Some of these essays go into more depth about an individual goddess than others, in particular Ereshkigal, Nephthys and Morgan le Fay. This is because the myths of these goddesses are often misinterpreted and exploring their story in full may reveal insights that may be contrary to popular public opinion. At the end of this section is the important return to the Upper World.

The third section of the book includes ideas of how to work with the goddesses on a more personal level by setting up a sacred altar, crafting masks and mirrors, specific spells and rituals that utilise the power of the dark and waning phases of the moon. Also included are instructions on how to make oils and incenses that will aid your working with each of the Dark Goddesses as well as exploration of the Shadow Self. At the end of the third section I offer additional suggestions when it

Nephthys by Soror Basilisk

# Part I

# The Dark Goddess

# Who is the Dark Goddess?

*"The goddess or Divine Mother holds the key to the spiritual*
*regeneration of humanity in this ecological age. Without reconnecting*
*to the deeper feminine energy of the universe, we are unlikely to*
*solve our current global crisis that is based, to a greater extent,*
*upon ignoring the divine presence of the goddess in nature and in*
*ourselves."*[11]

When the goddess is talked about with modern Pagan and
goddess-centric spiritual traditions, she is often referred to
in her triple form as Maiden, Mother and Crone, with each
aspect associated with a phase of the moon. This connection
between the goddess and the moon was first made by Jane Ellen
Harrison[12] and later mentioned by Robert Graves in his poetic
work, *The White Goddess*[13] as opposed to there being any actual
historical association. It is this latter aspect, the Crone, who
is commonly associated with the dark phase of the moon and
therefore the Dark Goddess. As the Crone, the Hag, she is the
older representative of the goddess who has passed her child-
bearing days and who now, through retaining her blood, retains
her wisdom. The Crone reminds us of our mortality, as it is she
who waits for us at the end of our days, where she will initiate
us into our new self only after showing us our transgressions
in this existence and subsequent lessons. Baba Yaga, Cerridwen
and Frau Holle are just some of the names given to the Crone.
However, they do not solely represent the Dark Goddess.

The late Shekhinah Mountainwater[14] used the term "Dark
Maiden" to describe the aspect of the goddess who is the
sorceress, the seducer, and the ruler of our suppressed desires.
Compared to the Crone, the Dark Maiden is young, sensual and
often enchantingly beautiful. She is Lilith, Circe and Persephone,
weaving her spells and illusions upon us. The Dark Maiden is

also the ferocious warrior who is not able to be controlled. These goddesses may or may not have consorts, a point that holds little importance when it comes to stepping into her own power. Here she is Sekhmet, Durga and Pele.

Probably the most terrifying aspect of all the goddesses is that of the "Dark" or "Terrible Mother", she who not only births us but also devours us. She shakes and destroys in order to transform and recreate, pushing us to our limits as if we need to prove to her (and ourselves) that we are "worthy". Her motherly love is "tough love" which we have little choice but to embrace. The lessons that the Dark Mother shows us are often realised through the process of reflection and contemplation. When the goddess appears in this form, she is known as Kali, Oya and Scathach. She sees straight through our veils or the masks that we wish to hide behind.

There are also many other aspects of the Dark Goddess who cannot easily be pigeonholed into the Maiden, Mother and Crone triplicity. This is because the Dark Goddess is the shapeshifter, the shadow stalker, who flits in and out of our dreams (or nightmares), stealing her way into our lives when we least expect it. She may reside in the Underworld, in the hidden depths of our subconscious, and in the shadowy realms just out of our peripheral vision, but she is also very much at home exposing herself (and our inner most fears) to the world, especially when we do not acknowledge her.

Should we continue to ignore her presence, her subtle communication and ways of getting our attention, she changes tactic and we find our lives "suddenly" (although it has never been sudden – we have just been ignoring the signs) collapsing around us. Be it through illness, stress, depression or another emotional crisis, even the realisation or total disbelief or dissatisfaction of our lives, the Dark Goddess has a way of getting our attention. According to Emma Restall Orr:

"... by her touch, we are woken to the darkness inside our own soul, allow us to better perceive - and at the same time reflecting – that which is all around us. Without sufficient reverence, we are lost."[15]

Orr goes on to remind us that while many religions tend to focus on the light, the actual source of all creativity, whether it be imagination or creation itself, is darkness. It is the dark womb of creation that is the core of woman, together with its currents and tidal flows of hormones, of blood, fertility, and emotion. This darkness is what makes a woman. It is her very nature and what is the centre of her creativity.[16]

Regardless of how we define her, it is the Dark Goddess who is often neglected or misunderstood. Orr further describes this aspect of the goddess as being the "formless unknown of complete release and pure potential within our souls"[17]. As such, we need to realise that it is within the darkness that the keys to the secrets and powers of the divine feminine can truly be found as well as our connection with the earth, the night, and the mysterious realm of dreams. It is within the darkness that a seed germinates and the brilliance of a star can be seen. Even magic and transformation take place here amongst the shadows. It is by understanding the Dark Goddess and integrating her into our spiritual lives that we can gain the true power of inner growth, not to mention the enlightenment of spiritual awareness.

# The Dark Goddess and the Shadow Self

*"It is a frightening thought that man also has a shadow side to him, consisting not just of little weaknesses and foibles, but of a positively demonic dynamism. The individual seldom knows anything of this; to him, as an individual, it is incredible that he should ever in any circumstances go beyond himself. But let these harmless creatures form a mass, and there emerges a raging monster."*[18]

The Dark Goddess is often associated with the "Shadow Self", a concept found within Jungian psychology. Carl Jung described the shadow as:

*"... a moral problem that challenges the whole ego-personality, for no one can become conscious of the shadow without considerable moral effort. To become conscious of it involves recognising the dark aspects of the personality as present and real. This act is the essential condition for any kind of self-knowledge, and it therefore, as a rule, meets with considerable resistance."*[19]

The Shadow Self is also seen as an archetype that represents the neglected side of our nature. It is this aspect of ourselves that can drag us down into a pit of despair. This "darker" side of our personality relates to the "reptilian", or our more primitive, instinctive brain functions that we share with all reptiles and mammals. These most powerful functions form part of our oldest coping brain functions and without which, we would not be alive. These functions include emotions and impulses such as anger (often coupled with fear), sex drive (need to procreate) and selfishness (survival). If any of these functions are taken to the extreme or enacted upon in a less than desirable manner (dictated by society's norms), then we may find ourselves shunned, our actions disproved of, and we end up being categorised as "undesirable".

According to psychotherapist David Richo, the shadow is:

"... that part of us that is incompatible with who we think we are or are supposed to be. It is the realm beyond our limits, the place where we are more than we seem. The shadow is ironically humorous because the opposite of our self-image proves to be true in spite of all our tricky attempts not to believe or display it. Fear of that wider self keeps it in the dungeon, but there are ways to release the prisoner."[20]

As humans are naturally social creatures, we tend to seek approval and acceptance into our "tribe" at some level. Therefore, to be, or have the fear of being, rejected can weigh heavy on our subconscious and cause devastating consequences. It is important to keep in mind that our modern Western society has largely been influenced by Christian morals for over 2,000 years which has impacted greatly on our subconscious, regardless of whether we perceive ourselves to be a Christian or not. The concept or fear of "guilt" should we demonstrate, or even realise we have, emotion-led behaviours that are deemed "inappropriate", or we do not live up to the expectations of others (usually a higher "authority") is an extremely heavy burden to carry. Regardless of whether it is engaging in promiscuous sex (usually attached to women more than to men), illicit drug taking, and alcohol abuse, or even choosing a different manner of parenting or diet, we can often find ourselves subjected to the disapproval and even be shamed by some sections of society. The negativity we are subjected to, no matter how much we attempt to ignore it, can lead to feelings of shame and guilt. These in turn may manifest into anxiety and depression. Our ever-changing social norms, when it comes to body image for example, have led to eating disorders, low self-esteem, self-harm and even drug addiction and personal shame. We are encouraged to seek an exceptionally high level of perfection with little thought given to the harm caused when we realise just how unattainable this level actual is, and we are sent tumbling.

In identifying with the Shadow Self and working with the Dark Goddess, we are able to understand that such behaviours may or may not be as guilt ridden as society portrays; that there are more appropriate and soul nourishing ways to express our negative emotions such as anger, and this society-perceived perfection is against our own natural state of being - as we are all perfect just the way we are.

When referring to the Dark Goddess only in the manner of the Shadow Self, there can be a danger in over-analysing our suffering, where we become a victim of circumstance and the blame is passed onto someone or something else (our parents, society, karma and the like). Such action does not free us from the "darkness", nor does it ultimately transfer responsibility to another. At the end of the day, how we act and continue to react to a situation or a person is our responsibility alone. The next time you observe yourself doing this, it might be interesting to ask yourself: "Does this action truly set me free or is it only a delaying tactic for the emotions waiting to be transformed?" Attempting to transfer our emotion to another does not sever our connection from the underlying cause.

As a representative of our Shadow Self, the Dark Goddess is an initiator, often at the deeper soul level; a psychopomp, leading us deep into the Underworld. She is also the ruler of the Underworld. This is her realm where her rules apply. As we will see in the following section, when it comes to working with the Dark Goddess it is quite common for the ancient Sumerian myth of the "Descent of Inanna" to be mentioned. This is because of the strong symbolic nature of this myth that we will see from the following retelling of it.

## Inanna's Descent into the Underworld

There are many ways to work with the Dark Goddess, either in individual aspects as outlined in the following section, or as a collective whole. With respect to the latter, this aspect of the divine feminine usually (but not always) follows the process that the Sumerian goddess Inanna took when she descended into the Great Below, the Underworld, the shadowy realms of Ereshkigal, who is often depicted as her older sister. The story of Inanna's descent comes from one of the earliest epic poems ever recorded, composed some time between 3,500 and 1,900 BCE (maybe even earlier). It consists of some 415 lines written on terracotta cuneiform tablets and is told from the perspective of Inanna's handmaiden, Ninshubur, whose own name means Queen of the East. While this myth is covered briefly in the essay about Ereshkigal that recounting specially addresses things from the Dark Goddess's point of view, her story, and not that of the descent that Inanna herself takes.

Due to the strong symbolic nature of Inanna's descent the story is often used. A popular modern translation of the myth can be found in *Inanna, Queen of Heaven and Earth: Her Stories and Hymns from Sumer*[21]. A brief recounting of the myth is as follows.

For reasons not made clear, Inanna, the Sumerian Queen of Heaven, decides to enter the Great Below, the realm of her sister, Ereshkigal, as the poem opens with the lines:

"From the great heaven she set her mind on the great below.
From the great heaven the goddess set her mind on the great below.
From the great heaven Inanna set her mind on the great below.
My mistress abandoned heaven, abandoned earth, and descended to the underworld."[22]

Aware that the Underworld was a place that no one could return from, before her descent, Inanna advises Ninshubur what she proposes to do and that should she not be able to escape after three days and three nights then the handmaiden is to beg Enlil (God of the Air and Inanna's father), Nanna (God of the Moon), and Enki (God of Wisdom) to bring her back.

Inanna dresses in her finery and gathers together the "Me", the holy laws of heaven and earth, which she has transformed into various items intended serve as protection from the Anunnaki, judges of the Underworld: her crown, earrings of small lapis beads, a double strand of beads about her neck, her breastplate called "Come, man, come", her golden hip girdle, the lapis measuring rod and line, and her royal breechcloth. Inanna then begins her descent.

When she arrives at the first of seven gates to the Great Below, Inanna finds it locked so she bangs on it, insisting the gate to be opened. When the gatekeeper Neti demands she identify herself and state her reason for wanting to enter the land from which no traveller returns, Inanna is taken aback that she is not recognised dressed in her finery. The Queen of Heaven advises that her desire to enter is:

"Because of my older sister, Ereshkigal,
Her husband, Gugalanna, the Bull of Heaven, has died
I have come to witness the funeral rites."[23]

She also lets Neti know that she has all the "Me" in her possession.

Neti leaves Inanna at the gate while he goes to let Ereshkigal know of her arrival. The Queen of the Dead is furious of what she perceives to be an interruption. She orders Neti to lock all the gates, and only allow Inanna entry after she relinquishes an item that connects her to the Upper World at each gate. At the first gate Inanna asks for the meaning of this indignity, to which Neti replies:

"Quiet, Inanna, the ways of the Underworld are perfect.
They may not be questioned."[24]

Having removed her crown, she comes to the second gate and is confronted with the same demand. When asked for the reason, Neti repeats his early answer that "the ways of the Underworld are perfect". At each gate Inanna arrives at, she is told again and again that the only way she is able to gain entry is by relinquishing an item of status. Each time she voices her objection it is always meet with the same simple yet firm statement: "The ways of the Underworld are perfect." It is clear that despite her regal status and finest of clothes, if Inanna wished to gain entry to the Great Below, even she, the Queen of Heaven, must abide by the rules. There are simply no exceptions.

Finally, Inanna arrives at the seventh gate and after relinquishing her royal breechcloth she passes through the final gate "naked and bent low". Once in the Great Below Inanna is quickly reminded she is not in control. She is surrounded by the Anunnaki, the seven judges of the Underworld, who pass judgement against her. Then she faces her sister, Ereshkigal, who:

"... fastened on Inanna the eye of death
She spoke against her the word of wrath
She uttered against her the cry of guilt
She struck her.
Inanna was turned into a corpse
A piece of rotting meat
And was hung from a hook on the wall."[25]

This is where Inanna remains for three days and three nights until Ninshubur raises the alarm that the Queen of Heaven is lost in the Underworld.

We will continue with the story of Inanna in the "Rising

from the Underworld" section at the end of Part II. For now, we analyse this first part of Inanna's descent and why it is important. It is Inanna's journey through the seven gates, the (internal) challenges she is faced, through being made to remove a status symbol, and her subsequent treatment in the Underworld that symbolises much of what working with the Dark Goddess is about. This is probably why this particular myth is often re-enacted. Being forced to release something that our ego self considers to be of importance including the stripping away of labels and external "safety nets" we tend to rely upon, as opposed to venturing into our own inner darkness and facing the truth about who we really are. Inanna is forced to do this over a period of three days and nights that she is hanging on the meat hook.

The story of Inanna can be perceived symbolically, as the seven gates she passes through can represent the seven major planets found within our solar system or the seven major chakras (energy systems found within the human body). This is because the number seven is considered to be an important number within many cultural groups. The seven specific items Inanna wears and has to relinquish at each gate are also interpreted as symbolic and rituals, based on Inanna's descent, enable participants to construct an item to reflect that which Inanna is forced to leave at each gate and to contemplate what that specific item means to them. For example, her crown could relate to our personality, the outward appearance that we show to the world, that we identify our outer self with.

While Robert Wilson[26] lists some different items that Inanna (or Ishtar as he refers to Inanna as) relinquishes, he relates them to various aspects of the Self. At the first gate Inanna surrenders her sandals instead of her crown which symbolises her will. At the second gate it is her jewelled anklets that relate to the ego. Her robe is surrendered at the third gate, which Wilson states is the hardest of all, because it means giving up mind itself. At the fourth gate Inanna surrenders her golden breast cups, representing her sexual role or sexuality. Her necklace is given up the fifth gate, representing giving up the rapture of illumination. The earrings at the sixth gate are her magic. And finally, at the seventh gate, Inanna surrenders her crown, her goddesshead. It is only then, once naked, that Inanna can enter eternity.

There is a domino effect when approaching and going through such work as well. The Dark Goddess touches our lives and everything that matters to us. This can be our relationships (both intimate as well as friendships and work colleagues), work and career, health, finances, home security, and so on. All these areas can effectively be lost when we work with the Dark Goddess. This is because she purges things that are not working from our lives, no matter how we may attempt to convince ourselves that they are. This purging is not without reason. It makes way for evolution and eventually renewal and re-emergence of the self that is in closer alignment with our soul's desire and objective in this incarnation.

When working with the Dark Goddess it is important to realise there is no "one size fits all". We will all have different experiences – some may appear "light" depending on how much inner/deeper spiritual work we have previously done, or what level of challenges our soul feels we are able to cope with. For other people however, it can be a deep cavern that has opened up, into which they have fallen.

Some people can integrate with their "new selves" relatively quickly and with a degree of ease. For others, however, this integration can take longer and may even involve several descents into the Underworld. The return journey may even reveal a completely different upper world. The only constant is the change that occurs to all who have journeyed this way.

# Descent, Death and the Dark Goddess

Any descent, regardless of whether it is voluntary or forced, can result in rather intense emotions. As with Inanna's story, her voluntary descent (i.e., where the choice was her own) resulted in her death as Ereshkigal fixed her "death glare" upon her and where Inanna's corpse was hung on a hook for three days and three nights.

The only difference between a voluntary and involuntary descent is often our sense of control. When we have decided to descend, even if we do not like the journey, it was our choice to start with. On the other hand, when we find ourselves tumbling down what seems to be the rabbit hole in Alice in Wonderland, then our journey can be made even more difficult as we scrabble in our attempt to grab hold (or control) of the life, or aspects of our life, we once knew.

During the last ten or so years that I have been working with and teaching about the Dark Goddess I have found myself involuntarily journeying into her realm on various occasions. While I do go into more detail about these journeys later in this book, the most recent descent, and the most profound, commenced in 2015 when I was diagnosed with cancer. It appears to be relevant to mention this journey here due to the far-reaching effects I endured and still continue to endure today.

The type of treatment recommended for my cancer lasted some 18 months and when it ended, so did my long term relationship, along with other aspects of my life. In fact, the more I attempted to re-assimilate myself back into the "normal" world, the more restless and out of place I felt. I often felt like Alice tumbling down the rabbit hole. Every time I tried to grasp hold of something from my past that would offer me a degree of stability, it felt as if I was being forced to let it go. Being out of control, the only option remaining for me was to "trust the process" as there were greater forces at play. I was learning to ride the waves while frantically trying to paddle against the current. It was only after an attempt to reconnect with my spirituality (that has always been a driving force in my life) that I was able to surrender to the roller coaster journey that I had been on, yet through my "busyness", had not totally embraced.

Many of the stable markers in my life were being dissolved. In the same way as Inanna was forced to relinquish parts of her identify at each gate, I also found myself relinquishing aspects of myself that I had built up over the last 20 years as they were no longer relevant to what was to come - losing my health, my career, my self-identity, my long hair, various friendships and more intimate relationships, the connection I had with my spirituality, and even those who I had considered to be my spiritual family. It was as if I was being forced to watch my life as I knew it slip slowly and often painfully through my fingers like grains of sand. As friendships faltered, I started to withdraw and shut myself off from the people around me. Turning inward was a form of self-preservation which seemed to be the only way I was going to make it through what was happening to me. I was in survival mode. When my treatment had finished and I was given a clean bill of health, it seemed to me that I was expected to be my "old self" again and carry on as if nothing had happened. But something had happened. The "old me" no longer existed. I felt I was treading water, likening myself to being a cork bobbing in the ocean, helpless against the endless waves. People around me did not seem to be able to understand or even appreciate what I was still going through. After all, I was now deemed "healthy", my cancer eradicated, so I should get over being sick.

Almost as an act of denial, I kept myself busy as I went through chemotherapy and radiotherapy treatment. My doctor had advised I cease working so I undertook study and volunteer work. In hindsight, this decision was detrimental in the long run as I never allowed myself time to grieve the losses in my life. It was only when my life nearly fell apart that I allowed myself to grieve. And grieve I did – not once, but over and over again, as many of the things (and people) I had held precious and dear to me were lost.

I now know grieving is a natural part of the descent process regardless of whether it is involuntary due to health reasons or voluntary. Seeing the descent and what you are prepared to give up, or are forced to give up, as "little deaths" is a much healthier and more beneficial way to deal with the process in the long run that is often overlooked.

When something, or an aspect of yourself "dies", we experience an element of. As Swiss psychiatrist Elizabeth Kűbler-Ross[27] points out, grief is not solely experienced by those who have lost a loved one. It can be experienced when you have lost a job, the ending of a relationship, having a beloved pet die, dealing with drug or alcohol addiction, or even through dealing with a chronic illness. Kűbler-Ross asserts there are five stages of experiencing grief:

**Denial**: Hanging onto the hope that the diagnosis or issue has been a mistake or is not true. Choosing to ignore toxic or negative behaviour in a partner, believing a relationship will miraculously heal itself. When we deny the grief, we are attempting to convince ourselves that all is right in the world when it is not.

**Anger**: Frustration and anger occurs when the denial cannot continue. "Why is this happening to me?" or "What have I done to deserve this?" is common especially when faced with a chronic illness.

**Bargaining**: When a change in lifestyle or compromise is hoped to avoid the current situation, or to alter the outcome in some way, maybe even to extend life for a diagnosis that is terminal.

**Depression:** Resolving that this is "one's lot" where a person withdraws from friends and society, becoming a recluse, inwardly mourning, burdening themselves with guilt and regrets.

**Acceptance:** The reality of the situation is embraced; one's mortality is realised and retrospection is undertaken. Plans are made for the future as you are no longer looking backwards to the past and what had been, but to the future and what there possibly could be.

If we do not allow ourselves to grieve naturally after our descent and release our attachment to what has been lost, then our ability to return to the surface and completely integrate our new life can be difficult.

At each gate that Inanna arrives at she was force to relinquish an aspect of herself that related to her persona, her status, her outward self. One of the hardest things we often find is that we are forced to release what we are not familiar or comfortable with. Ask yourself: what will you give up should the Dark Goddess ask you to give something up? Will it be your beauty or good looks? Your work or family? How about friends, pets, your work or career, health, personality, identity in the world, financial security, children?

There is no bargaining with the Underworld as Inanna soon discovers. Likewise, we cannot hang onto things that are in need of change or expect things to change if we are stuck in the past, or even the present. For some people the comfortable and the familiar is always a "safer" option, regards of how detrimental it may be, when compared with the unknown and the less familiar. For other people, being in a relationship, regardless of the situation or how they are being treated, is better than being alone.

Little do we realise, however, all external relationships, likewise happiness, peace, quality of life etc is merely a reflection of our inner world. In order to have a successful relationship with another person should we first not have a successful relationship with our own self?

If you are not able to say "yes" to the surrender, then spend time contemplating why:

- What is the attachment? Is it justified or based on fear?
- Where does this fear originate? Is it justified or has it been based on something else, or even a pre-conceived belief?
- Does that pre-conceived belief help or hinder you, your spiritual growth, etc?

There are people who have never felt that "out of control" feeling that an involuntary descent in the Underworld can bring. After the first six or so years of working with the Dark Goddess through the running of rituals and workshops, I felt almost immune to her. That was, until one day she reached up and dragged me down into her realm and I found myself on the banks of a river wallowing in self-pity while attending a conference. The aspect of the Dark Goddess who came through was not one from any myth, but resembled an image from a tarot deck, a Celtic leather clad warrior woman who viewed me with a degree of what I can only describe as disapproval for allowing myself to be sucked into the ego-driven battles that were happening around me. "Wear your crown", she told me, meaning for me to stand in my own power, and regardless of whether I remained on the outside, I needed to continue doing my "work" in the way I felt driven to do.

One thing my journeys with the Dark Goddess have enforced upon me is that death is not the end – it leads to rebirth. There have been several occasions when it has been necessary to consider myself as a caterpillar, lying in a state of rest inside its cocoon awaiting transformation into a magnificent butterfly. Regardless of whether your descent is voluntary or involuntary, when you are spiralling down into the Underworld it can be beneficial to keep in mind that you too are going through a transformation process where you will be morphed into a new state, even a new identity. Pause for a moment and consider what you or your soul desires to transform into?

Keep in mind that from decaying compost sprouts new life. Night becomes day. Decay provides important nutrients that enhance and enable the next stage in the endless cycle that is life. Not all changes are immediate. Often you will only notice them over the following weeks or months when things you once considered important to you no longer appear to be. It is important to set boundaries around your new self to enable you the opportunity to spend time with and on the most important person in your life – you. This is because not everyone in your life will be open and willing to embrace the new you.

The experience of a descent can be an extremely humbling experience. Inanna's descent forces her, the Queen of Heaven to realise she is not that important. In fact, in the Underworld she becomes quite insignificant. The same occurs to us. Do you honestly think the work will not get done, the bills will be unpaid, the meals not prepared etc if you did not do them? At the end of the day the sun will still rise and life will continue on regardless.

Hel by Soror Basilisk

# Descending into the Great Below

To truly understand the Dark Goddess is nearly impossible. Her darkness itself reflects back a depth that can be so profound it disturbs our psyche. Her appearance in our lives is often intense when we find ourselves standing before the unfathomable abyss, overcome with perturbed emotions, fear and apprehension as our world falls apart around us, and our control slips through our fingers like grains of sand. Yet she is there waiting. Instead of initially surrendering to the process, many of us attempt to hang on to the familiar, regardless of how detrimental it may be. It is only when we realise that to fight against this change and that hanging on is futile and is actually only adding to our pain and anguish that our only option is to completely surrender to the process, whatever that may be, and accept what we are undergoing. This does not necessarily mean the journey we find ourselves undertaking will be any less painful, but there does tend to be even a minute degree of clarity in the process, offering us the opportunity to breathe when we learn to ride the waves instead to attempting to battle against them.

The Dark Goddess appears when transformation is needed. This transformation, regardless of whether we are consciously aware of it or not, is often needed at a deeper level for our own soul's evolution. For this deep change to occur, unwanted or outdated habits, behaviours, situations or even relationships need to be shed. Emotional detachment can be experienced as we witness layers of our life being removed. Many of these layers have been moulded into us by other people's perceptions and society's expectations. If we are consciously aware of this, then there may be a degree of hesitation or reluctance on our part to make the necessary changes.

The Dark Goddess has no emotional attachment to the unwanted. She cannot be influenced by the needs and expectations of other people. She has no interest in gender, race, and politics. Men as well as women can work with the Dark Goddess. She goes beyond human layering and labels. What she focuses on is the deeper level change and transformation that is needed in our own life in order to bring about longer term positive results.

Of course, we could choose to ignore her existence and continue with the life that we are familiar with. However, in doing this it will only be a matter of time before she makes her presence known to us, storming into our lives and erupting like a volcano to ensure that our life will never be the same again. Often, rightly so, if we have been heading off down the "wrong" path or direction. The longer and stronger that we have ignored her, the stronger we hang onto our previous existence, the more powerful and the greater impact she will have on our life.

Regardless of how we define her, it is the Dark Goddess who tends to be neglected, feared or misunderstood. We need to realise that it is within the darkness that the keys to the secrets and powers of the divine feminine can truly be found, as well as our connection with the earth, night, and the mysterious realm of dreams. Even magic and transformation takes place here amongst the shadows. It is within the darkness that a seed germinates, and the brilliance of a star can be seen. It is within understanding the Dark Goddess and integrating her into our spiritual lives that we can gain the true power of inner growth, not to mention the enlightenment of spiritual awareness.

As already mentioned, my more recent journey into the Great Below, the realm of Ereshkigal, was forced, not volunteered. It came about through the diagnosis of cancer. For most of my adult life I have been naturally drawn to the Dark Goddess and her shadowy realms. Cancer, however, brought me to the first gate, the gate where everyone is forced to commence their journey downwards. No longer was I able to slip through the back door so to speak. For this is what the Dark Goddess does, reminds us of the unexpected, constantly testing our resolve, all with deeper purpose than what our conscious mind is comfortable with. It is she who calls to our deeper soul self, our higher consciousness, that has not been caught up or bogged down by ego-based connections and associations our physical self experiences – pain, grief, distress and other deep emotions. But such feelings are important to our own spiritual growth and soul development for it is through experiencing emotions, the "feeling" of pain, suffering etc, that our soul gains invaluable insights into ways as to how best to rise above such feelings and work through them in order to see the lessons that are contained within.

We do not need to wait for the Dark Goddess to call us. It can be just as beneficial for us to voluntarily enter her realm. Through exploring the myths and using the suggested meditations and other exercises provided in this book the separate aspects of the Dark Goddess can be individually worked with depending on our needs, or the reader can journey to meet the Dark Goddess as a collective. Each goddess mentioned within the pages of this book will challenge you in their own unique way to look beneath the surface and accept what is there, as well as encourage you to break free of conformity and outdated values. They wait for you to descend into their realm and to accept the terms as presented. Through the use of meditations and exercises provided in this book, these goddesses will entice you to step beyond your comfort zone in order to experience true freedom at a deep soul level, which will eventually free you from current restraints and/or restrictions, all adding to soul evolution and continual growth.

When approaching the Dark Goddess, especially ones from other cultures, often the biggest mistake people have is to focus on her external image, her impending darkness, upon which all the negativities of human nature are projected. Instead of looking at the darkness that these goddesses emanate as the supreme originating power, what is actually seen is one's own repressed emotions (such as hurt, abandonment, distrust or even rage), superstition and even primitive impulses. Many of the Dark Goddesses represent the expression of mystery. Kali, for example, is described as the "supreme power of the magical, awesome, cataclysmic universe in which we live"[28]. For her worshippers, Kali holds our life and death within her embrace and is the first, as well as the last, the beginning as well as the end of everything.

Working with the Dark Goddess can peel away the veil that has been preventing us, for whatever reason, from making the often uncomfortable, yet extremely necessary, changes in our lives. As we journey inward, we can undergo a process that within shamanic teachings is known as "soul retrieval". This process often occurs at a deep subconscious level and involves regaining, or even reclaiming, those aspects of the soul that have been lost or separated due to events in our lives up until this point. Once the fractured soul is retrieved or the previously mentioned shadow is acknowledged and integrated, we can become complete and perfectly whole – much like the Taoist yin/yang symbol. Once whole again, we find that we stop going around in circles and can attract more beneficial situations and people into our lives.

This is different from the phrase "finding yourself" that is often heard within a number of modem psychotherapies, for at the core of our being there is actually no "self" to find. Instead, there at our core is a place of nothingness, a void that allows for all potentiality to occur. This means we were never actually lost in the first place. In order to realise the potentiality that can manifest all we really need to do is to sit and breathe in this nothingness, and in doing so, we will be able to "find ourselves", and what, we are constantly being told, is missing in our lives.

Light can be a blinding illusion, distraction from the truth, preventing us from seeing the reality that is in front of us. The Dark Goddess does not appear in our lives to intentionally bring us pain. She delivers "tough love" that brings us the ultimate truth, which can result in the realisation of the negative patterns we create for ourselves, the negative choices we make, and how it is up to us, no one else, to make the change.

At the end of the day, we cannot have light without darkness. It is only within the darkness that possibilities are revealed and miracles linger, where renewal can happen, leading to rebirth to occur.

Working with the Dark Goddess calls for truth. Not our perceived truth but the Truth, the universal truth that is not hidden behind our rose-tinted emotionally enhanced glasses. She projects images of us that we often do not wish to acknowledge, let alone accept. Our journey into her realm is to discover who she really is, to lift the veil and see what lies beneath, and to come face to face with her. This is because the goddess, in all her guises, is reflected within each of us. When we work with, acknowledge and embrace the Dark Goddess, we also work with, acknowledge and embrace those hidden or ignored aspects within our own self.

Just as there are many aspects of the Dark Goddess so too are there many ways of working with these aspects. My personal experience has been a combination of voluntarily descending into the Underworld as well as being dragged in to the Great Below, like Kore (Persephone), when the Dark Goddess has appeared unannounced. When the latter occurs, it is very much as if she begins to unravel the threads that make up our lives. Depending on how spiritually open or accepting we are, it can feel as if she stares deep within our soul watching for our reaction as the unravelling process takes place.

Even if our descent is voluntary, once the unravelling commences there is no way of stopping it. It is a creation process in itself. The best advice I can give is simply to breathe and surrender to the process. After all this is what you have wanted, what you needed, even if that desire was on a deep subconscious level. From personal experience it feels like being Alice falling down the rabbit warren (on an easy descent), or being caught up in the agitation cycle of a washing machine (on a deeper, more soul wrenching descent). No two journeys are ever the same, for the purpose is to take you out of your comfort zone.

Journeying into the Underworld successfully calls for surrender, giving up control which can be extremely difficult to do if you are a control freak (or well organised planner as I prefer to call myself), or even a rather logical person - for what often happens will test your sanity, what you perceive as logical, your frontal lobe (the part of the brain that governs logical thinking) as well as your left brain (your more academic side).

A voluntary descent may be the best option, however, as we are dealing with deeper soul issues. Should our soul believe a lesson or change needs to occur, then we may find ourselves at the first gate to the Underworld where there is often no turning back.

Any resistance to the surrendering, to letting go and allowing the process to unfold, only increases the intensity. As soon as we release our grip and realise there is only one way we are heading (downward) then the process can (but not always) be easier, and may be less soul destroying as we loosen our grip on emotional attachments to things, situations, and even people that need to be released or removed from our lives.

Clinging onto things is normal. We are not often instructed or informed about the Underworld process. Our Western culture tends to see such realms as evil, for the mentally unstable, or for the deprived, and yes, they can be. Yet, there is also an element of freedom as we detach and step away from perceived social, cultural and even family expectations and restraints.

The "ways of the Underworld are perfect" Inanna gets told over and over again. We may not see this perfection at the time because it is masked by other emotions (pain, guilt, sadness, loss, anger, etc).

We are forced to release, relinquish, and are stripped of something that is of important to us each time we descend. If it is a voluntary descent then we may have a degree of choice about what this thing of value that we are about to lose from our life may be, what we are prepared to lose, to sacrifice.

If the descent is not voluntary, or at least we are aware of it on a conscious level, then that is a different ball game. The more we resist, the harder our descent becomes. If we operate from a place of victim mentality, "poor me", for example then instances will present themselves in our lives that will indicate we need to relinquish this limiting belief, a need to take responsibility for our own role in situations.

When working with the Dark Goddess it is important to realise that each are distinctly different from the other. It is important to spend time developing a relationship with one at a time in order to fully understand and experience the different personalities and energies.

All the various names and faces of the Dark Goddess represent the unknown change and even death (of the ego). She is the one who greets us at the end of our days as well as being the one who was with us at the beginning of time – even before time itself for, after all, she was the creator of time. She reminds us of what needs to be removed from our lives and will even commence the releasing process if we hesitate for too long. When we listen to her we will find that even amongst the chaos she offers a place where our soul can rest for deep healing to occur. Once this has taken place, the Dark Goddess guides us back through the gateway, allowing us to be reborn anew.

*The many guises of the Dark Goddess are waiting for you …*
*Are you brave enough to meet them?*

Ereshkigal by Soror Basilisk

# Part II

# Meeting the Dark Goddess

# Hail to the Dark Goddess

(Frances Billinghurst, 2016)

Hail to the Silent One
Who was here before time began
The one whose breath is felt upon the wind
Reminding us of her ever-reaching grip on our life
Spinning the fated wheel of life and death
And all which goes beyond.

Hail to the Dark One
Whose withered grasp brings disease and death
The shadow lurker of our nightmares
Reminding us of our fragile mortality
The cause of which is our birth
The cure is our demise.

Hail to the Terrible One
Forcing us to face reality
Who squashes our unrealistic dreams
Ignoring the spine chilling screams we make
As we realise our grasp is to be loosened
On this falsehood of reality.

Hail to the Wise One
Encouraging us to embrace pain and lick our wounds
Waiting for us to accept the true emotion
To realise that nothing is perfect and shit happens
But it is this that makes us stronger, that tests us.
The whirlwind of change that stalks us
From the shadows.

Hail to the Strong One
Who demands us to stand on our own feet
To reclaim our power and our truth
Even if we feel alone – but we are never this.
She is always watching, waiting.
The darkness from which light emerges
The comforting shadow when we feel all is lost
She is the embrace that takes us home.

Hail the Ungracious One
Who speaks her mind and releases her feelings
Instead of swallowing the pain
She is our anger and our outrage
Demanding that we embrace the power
Bubbling from deep within our core.

Gracious Mother of the Darkness
Whose fear we experience is the fear of our ignorance
Reminding us of the hidden truth of the true self
Laying it before us – naked and bare
The peace revealed when we finally understand
She is not separate from us.
She is us.
We are one.

# Thirteen Aspects of the Dark Goddess

Over the years I have worked with individual aspects of the Dark Goddess (including those who appear within this book), the Dark Goddess as a collective concept (as opposed to an aspect), and even involuntarily when I have found myself likened to the Sumerian goddess Inanna arriving at the first gate to the Underworld. The reasons why I have worked with this aspect of the divine feminine, as opposed to utilising other techniques, have been varied. Due to my interest in Jungian psychology the use of myth to gain a deeper insight into my own subconscious has proven most beneficial, as well as being congruent with another interest of mine, that of metaphysics.

I have felt drawn to these "dark", more mysterious and more commonly lesser understood aspects of the divine feminine, possibly because I felt akin to them, that maybe they reflected my introverted nature.

For those of us who feel we have journeyed with her aspects for many years we can suddenly find ourselves out of control. Just because you have worked with the Dark Goddess once or in one format, or even under the guidance of one particular teacher does not mean you have completely embraced all of your shadow qualities and therefore no longer need to undergo such work. It does not take you off the Dark Goddess's radar. From my own experience working with the Dark Goddess tends to be a never-ending exposure to the different levels of my soul, an experience that commenced some 25 or so years ago.

Working with the Dark Goddess does not necessarily mean you are not working with a lighter aspect of the goddess, the divine feminine, either. As mentioned earlier, these are just labels we humans give the goddess. She is beyond them.

What is covered in the following pages is a selection of 13 aspects of the Dark Goddess, together with their myths, to assist you in getting to know their stories. Each section about the individual goddesses also includes an activity or meditation to further help you in establishing a relationship with them, or an exercise that will enable you to connect with their energy on a deeper level.

Building up a personal relationship with the goddess you are working with is by far one of the more recommended way of working with deity, in my view. This is done through the act of devotion where you are establishing a relationship with deity, through research or using your own intuition, discovering traditional connections and offerings, reciting prayers, mantras, and so on.

Remember, these 13 goddesses appear in no particular order and you are welcome to pick and choose any or all that you are drawn to work with.

For readers who would like to undergo a longer and more in-depth journey with the different aspects of the Dark Goddess, details about workshops, including both the physical and online sadhanas (sacred practice), can be found towards the end of this book.

# Tiamat: The Original Creatrix

*When there was no heaven,*
*No earth, no height, no depth, no name,*
*When Apsu was alone,*
*The sweet water, the first begetter;*
*and Tiamat the bitter water, and that*
*Return to the womb, her Mummu,*
*When there were no gods –*
*When sweet and bitter*
*Mingled together, no reed was plaited*
*No rushes muddied the water,*
*The gods were nameless natureless, futureless.*[29]

The Babylonian creation myth, the *Enuma Elish*[30] (the "Seven Tablets of Creation"), is considered to be the oldest recorded creation myth known, dating to at least 2,000 BCE. It was believed to have been recited publicly during the fourth day of the festival of Akitu, the Babylonian new year, to remind the people of their origin, where all creation rose from the mingling of two primal waters: the sweet waters (deified as the god Abzu, more commonly referred to as the later Akkadian Apsu) and the salt waters (deified as the goddess Tiamat).

Abzu ("the Begetter") and Tiamat (the "Mother of All Things") were the original divine couple from whom everything else came into creation. The first of the great gods created from the "mingling" of their waters was Mummu, the God of Spray, as well as two serpent gods, Lahmu and Lahamu. From these, more gods were created, including Ea (the Sumerian god Enki, patron of the ancient city of Eridu, who was Lord of Earth and the Waters), who later became the chief Babylonian god.

According to the *Enuma Elish*, as more and more gods were created, they began communicating with each other with a type of speech that Abzu found annoying, for it disturbed the peace. He commented to Tiamat that in order for peace to be restored, the younger gods needed to be destroyed. This suggestion horrified Tiamat[31] who managed to convince Abzu to give the younger gods another chance. It was not long before Abzu found his peace disturbed again and he began plotting the killing of the younger gods. This time, however, Ea became aware of Abzu's scheme and through the use of magic, managed to put his grandfather into a trance so he could kill him. It was from Abzu's body that Ea made his home.

The killing of Abzu angered Tiamat's scorpion-headed son and champion, Qingu, who reported the incident back to Tiamat. Now depicted as a vengeful and terrifying monster in the *Enuma Elish*, Tiamat called to avenge the death of her beloved consort, and declared war against the younger gods. Her army of monsters included sea serpents, storm demons and fish-men. With Tiamat being a more formidable opponent than Abzu, the younger gods elected the untried Marduk, son of Ea, to be their hero against her.

Prior to the battle, Tiamat handed Qingu the Tablet of Destiny that contained the pre-ordained divine decrees. This tablet legitimised the rule of a god and controlled the fates.[32] But wearing it as a breastplate did not prevent Marduk from killing Qingu and obtaining the Tablet of Destiny for himself. Such an action installed Marduk as the ruler of all of the Babylonian gods.

Marduk then incited Tiamat into one-on-one combat. Harnessing a team of four horses to his chariot, the young ruler rushed towards the "fierce dragoness", raising flood waters as he rode. She tried to swallow her attacker but instead became entangled in his net. Into her face, Marduk threw the storm wind, and when Tiamat opened her mouth, he forced the wind inside of her, filling her stomach. Ensnared and now bloated, Tiamat was not able to move. Marduk quickly fired an arrow into her now swollen body, killing her.

With great force Marduk cut out Tiamat's heart, crushed her skull, and then split her great body into two halves. Marduk rose up one half of Tiamat's body into the sky, from which he made the heavens, stations in the stars for the gods, and the moon which he set on its course across the heavens. He also posted guard to ensure Tiamat's salty waters would not escape. The other half of Tiamat's body became the earth which Marduk placed over Abzu's fresh waters. From her weeping eyes, the two great rivers, the Tigris and the Euphrates, were created, mist from her spittle and mountains from her breasts.[33] Thus, from the body of the "Mother of All Living Things", Marduk was recorded as having created the heavens as "out of chaos, came order."

There are many interpretations of Tiamat's myth with some even indicating she is actually a deity much older than the *Enuma Elish* and even the Babylonian people, that being Nammu, the goddess of the earlier Sumerian people. Nammu was considered to be the primeval sea who gave birth to An (heaven) and Ki (the earth). Whilst Tiamat was associated with the creation of the universe, she was also depicted as being the universe herself, a more primal deity who stemmed back to a time of chaos, before life itself was created. This is one of the two reasons why Tiamat is considered to be a Dark Goddess, being the original creatrix, not only of the universe but also of the younger race of gods.

It is unfortunate that today, when her myth is told, the focus tends to be on Tiamat's anger and revenge (the second reason why she is classified as a Dark Goddess), and the subsequent siding of the younger gods with Marduk that resulted in her destruction. However, destruction is needed for new creation to be made. As in the case of Tiamat, this new creation came in the form of the earth beneath our feet and the vast skies above us.

## Working with Tiamat
Within modern Paganism and goddess-centric spiritualties, Tiamat is associated with chaos, birth/creation, and even death.

Being a dragon-like creature of chaos, a sea serpent from the primordial waters, she brings forth change, especially at an extremely deep, or even more ancient level.

The salty watery abyss from which Tiamat originated can be likened with the salty watery seas that the human race emerged from. Coupled with her ancientness, this makes Tiamat the perfect goddess to work with when it comes to tackling deep rooted issues, even discovering the source of such issues that form the core of our being, such as cultural perceptions we know are long outdated yet are not able to shake off, or stubborn habits that need changing at a cellular level.

As creatrix of the heavens, Tiamat represents our core self, our higher consciousness, the divine spark that lives on way past the life span of the physical body has expired. As creatrix of the earth, she represents the "bones" of our existence.

## Invocation to Tiamat

Hail to thee, O Mother of the Cosmic Void
From whose slain body created the heavens and the earth
You hold the Universe in your coiled embrace
For yours are the sacred keys to the kingdom of all knowledge.
Your timeless essence is the soul of the world,
Your blood is the vital force of every living being.
Tiamat, dragon goddess of creation and destruction,
You who are more ancient than time.
Arise up from the Cosmic Void and come to me.

## Correspondences associated with Tiamat

Dragons, the sea/ocean, waves, shells (in particular deep-water ones), dragon's blood jasper, ocean jasper, amazonite or moldavite, coral, blue and green colours, dragon's blood resin, salt water, the cosmos, the Milky Way.

## Meditation: Connection with the Original Creatrix

The following meditation is to take you back to the primordial waters, before all life was created, in order to realign yourself with this original aspect of the Great Goddess. To begin, ensure you are in an appropriate position and environment for meditation. If the concept of meditation is not new to you, then you may wish to skip the following few sentences.

Close your eyes and relax, focusing on your breath as you inhale and exhale, inhale and exhale. If you find your thoughts start to wander, bring them back to watching the breath. When you feel your body and mind is relaxed, bring your awareness to your contact point with the ground beneath you. If you are sitting in a chair, then this will be your feet. If you are sitting on the ground, then this will be your lower coccyx or the base of your spine. With each breath that you take, visualise, or imagine, you are drawing energy up from the ground, from Mother Earth.

If you are familiar with the concept of the chakras (energy centres), then draw the energy up through your muladhara (base) chakra located at the base of your spine, then into your svadhisthana chakra (located at your sacral area, about 5 cm below your navel), manipura chakra (just above your navel), anahata (heart) chakra, vishuddha (throat) chakra, ajna (third eye between the eye brows) chakra, and finally up and out through the sahasrara (crown) chakra at the top of your head. If the concept of chakras is unfamiliar then simply imagine you are drawing the energy up through your spinal column and out through the top of your head and releasing it into the cosmos beyond.

Continue with this process of drawing in energy as you inhale, drawing it up through your spine and releasing it through the top of your head into the cosmos as you exhale for at least five minutes, or until you feel truly connected with the earth and the cosmos.

Beneath you is the source of earth energy that is your earth star. Above you, beyond your crown chakra, located at the top of your head, is your soul star, the origin of enlightenment, through which you connect with your higher self. Between the two, you are a channel of light and energy that connects both of these sources. As you continue to breathe, become aware that as you inhale light is flowing into your physical self from the earth star beneath you and from the soul start above you, through the stellar gateway into your physical body simultaneously, and mingling at your heart centre. As you exhale, the energies move throughout your body, along what are known as meridian lines, or nadis, filling every cell in your body with healing energy. As you breathe, visualise your physical form becoming lighter and brighter as more and more energy flows into and through it.

Beyond the soul star, in the distance away up in the cosmos, is a glittering light, the source of energy that is your being. As you breathe, feel your energetic body floating up through the stellar gate, passed your soul star and up into the cosmos towards this light. This is the primordial source of all beings, the watery realms of chaos, the ultimate source of creation. Continue to inhale and exhale allowing any insight from this original source to make its way to you.

When you feel that you have received as much insight as you need, slowly bring your awareness back to your physical self, closing off your connection to your soul and earth star, and then closing down your crown chakra and any other chakra centres that you have opened. With each breath that you take, bring your awareness more and more to your physical self, increasing your awareness to your physical surroundings, moving your fingers and toes. Open your eyes when you feel reconnected again.

# Sekhmet the Powerful

*Mine is a heart of carnelian, crimson as murder on a holy day.*
*Mine is a heart of cornel, the gnarled roots of a dogwood and the*
*bursting of flowers.*
*I am the broken wax seal on my lover's letters.*
*I am the phoenix, the fiery sun, consuming and resuming myself.*
*I will what I will.*
*Mine is a heart of carnelian, blood red as the crest of a phoenix.*[34]

Amongst the plethora of Egyptian gods, the lion headed goddess Sekhmet is more commonly known as the daughter of the sun god Ra and was associated with the intense blinding heat of the noontime sun. With her name deriving from the Egyptian word *sekhem* (meaning "power" or "might"), it is believed that Sekhmet may have pre-dated the Old Kingdom[35] gods as one of her epithets was: "One who was before the Gods", and may have even come to Egypt from neighbouring Sudan (where lions were plentiful). It was at Memphis (Men-nefer) in southern Egypt that her main centre of worship existed, and here she formed part of the divine triad along with her husband Ptah (the creator god who shaped the heavens and earth from his potter's wheel) and their son, Nefertem (who was closely associated with healing and healers).

When the power shifted from Memphis to Thebes during the New Kingdom[36], Sekhmet's attributes were absorbed into those of Mut (Amaunet), the vulture headed goddess who made up the Theban triad along with Amun and Khons. An example of this was evidenced by the erection of numerous lioness headed goddess statues by Amenhotep III[37] (Dynasty XVIII) in the precinct of Mut's temple ("isheru") south of the Great Temple of Amun at Karnak. The purpose of these statues was to receive offerings, with one statue being honoured on a particular day throughout the year. Amenhotep III also erected leonine statues at his own mortuary temple in western Thebes. Of the two goddesses, Sekhmet remains the better known.

Despite her being a feline (which has sometimes led to a modern misconception that Sekhmet was a more malignant aspect of the cat goddess Bast), it was as the wrathful form of Hathor (the cow headed goddess of joy, dance and birth) that Sekhmet was more commonly associated. A temple at Kom el-Hisn in the western Delta was dedicated to both Hathor and Sekhmet, and at his temple at Abydos, Seti I (a ruler during Dynasty XIX) was pictured being suckled by Hathor with the title "Mistress of the Mansion of Sekhmet".

It is as the "Eye of Ra" that Sekhmet is commonly known. In this role, she meted out divine punishment to the enemies of the gods as his earthly representative. According to *The Myth of the Destruction of Mankind* (engraved upon one of the shrines belonging to boy king Tutankhamen), Ra took on the form of a man and became the first pharaoh of Egypt. In this capacity he ruled over the country for thousands of years, and during that time great harvests were achieved. As a human, this meant Ra was subjected to growing old, as do all mortals, and eventually people grew less fearful of him and ceased obeying his laws and commands. In fact, they started to laugh at him, mocking him with words such as: "Look at Ra. His bones are like silver, his flesh like gold, his hair is the colour of lapis lazuli."

This mockery angered Ra, along with the evil deeds that were being done in defiance of his laws. He called together all the gods that he had made, these being Shu (air), Tefnut (moisture), Geb (earth) and Nut (sky), and summoned Nun (the primordial waters and original chaos). As mankind continued to jeer at Ra and break his laws, Ra addressed Nun:

"Eldest of the gods, you who made me; and you gods whom I have made: look upon mankind who came into being at a glance of my eye. See how men plot against me; hear what they say of me; tell me what I should do to them. For I will not destroy mankind until I have heard what you advise."

Nun replied:

"My son Ra, the god greater than he who made him and mightier than those whom he has created, turn your mighty eye upon them and send destruction upon them in the form of your daughter, the goddess Sekhmet."

At the terrible glance from the Eye of Ra, Sekhmet, the fiercest of all goddesses, came into being. At the bidding of Ra, she slays all the people who had scorned and disobeyed him. Rejoicing in the slaughter, Sekhmet took pleasure in the taste of blood, and every night she reported back to Ra how many people she had killed.

Night after night the Nile River ran red with blood as Sekhmet went through the land slaying everyone in sight. The more people she killed, the more blood she drank, and this increased her thirst for even more blood. Ra soon realised that no one could stop Sekhmet, not even the sun god himself. And the only way she would cease slaying people would be of her own accord, which, as Ra realised, could only come about through a degree of cunning.

Seven thousand jars of a strong barley beer called "sleep maker" were mingled with red ochre from Elephantine (in southern Egypt) and resembled the blood of men when it glistened in the moonlight. The jars were taken to the place where Sekhmet proposed to slay men when the sun rose and were poured over the fields. When Sekhmet arrived at the site, she found no living creature, yet the ground was covered in what she thought was blood. Believing it to be so, she drank until she could no longer slay. Reeling back to where Ra was waiting, she announced she had not been able to kill even a single man.

"You come in peace, sweet one," Ra said, changing her name to Hathor, and her nature was also changed to the sweetness of love and the strength of desire.

As the "Protectress of the Divine Order", Sekhmet not only protected the gods against evil forces, including disobedience, but she also protected anything she was responsible for. She was adopted by the Egyptian pharaohs as a symbol of their own unvanquishable heroism in battle, where she aided by launching fiery arrows, or even breathing fire, at their enemies, as in the Battle of Kadesh where she was pictured on the horses of Ramesses II with her flames scorching the bodies of the enemy soldiers. Within the *Pyramid Text* there is mention that a king or pharaoh was conceived by Sekhmet herself.

A further epithet was "Lady of Pestilence", as spells existed whereby Sekhmet was called upon to send plagues and disease against enemies, which were delivered by "messengers" of Sekhmet. Her ability to do this also meant she could be invoked to avoid plague and cure disease, and as the "Lady of Life", Sekhmet was also known to counteract illness, with her priesthood seemingly having a prophylactic role in medicine.

## Working with Sekhmet

In modern times, Sekhmet can appear to have been reinvented into a rather benign force, even being worshipped as a "gentle mother". Regardless how we may perceive her today, it is important to keep in mind that to the ancient Egyptians she was dangerous and ferocious, the bringer of plagues and retribution, and the fire of the sun god's eye. While Sekhmet can still be approached as a healer, a bringer of justice and as a guardian or protector, this should be done with respect and caution as she is an extremely powerful force.

Sekhmet is also perceived as a source of strength, independence and assertiveness. While she may appear to be an appropriate symbol of the modern woman, as a healer, bringer of justice and as a guardian or protector, Sekhmet is still far from being a benign figure that could be adored and worshipped as a gentle mother. This lion-headed goddess of the Egyptian sun is still the force of chaos and can be as ferocious in her bringing of "plagues and retribution" today as she was in ancient Egypt. It is this aspect of Sekhmet that aligns her as an aspect of the Dark Goddess.

## Invocation to Sekhmet

I beseech thee, O Powerful One!
She who is the daughter of Ra
She who is the life-giver to the Gods
Lady of Rekht, Lady of Pekhet, Lady of Set
Lady of Rehesaui, Lady of Tchar and of Sehert
Hail to thee, O Sekhmet, Lady of the Flame
Whose name is known for eternity.
It is you, O Mother in the Horizon of Heaven,
Goddess of Wars and Destroyer of Rebellions
Deliver me from the Abode of Fiends.
I seek thee, O powerful Sekhmet
So mighty is thy name,
Come and reveal thyself to me.

## Correspondences associated with Sekhmet

Lions, the desert, sun, sand, solar disks, Eye of Ra, orange carnelian, ruby, garnet, emerald, gold, frankincense and myrrh resin, sandalwood, rose, red and orange colours, beer (amber ale), red wine, menstrual blood.

## Exercise: Releasing Anger

One interpretation of the myth of Sekhmet implies that she is associated with the emotion of anger. For most of us, anger is an emotion we take within. When anger is pushed into the shadows and not dealt with, it does not go away – it waits until one day it erupts, spewing forth unexpectedly, rather like a volcano blowing its top. Hidden or repressed anger is a great energy drain, and can even manifest itself through other means, the more common of which being depression.

Anger can dominate our thinking and we can very often lose sight of who we are actually angry at. Are we angry with someone because they have pushed our buttons, or because they mirror something that we dislike about ourselves?

It is easier to attribute blame to someone else, letting that serve as a distraction from the root cause within the self. Rage has a way of adhering on the cellular level, causing mind and body damage. Emotional damage is readily observable as are some of the physiological effects: rapid heartbeat and acid secretion due to the fight or flight response. However, the rage that is forever housed in our cells returns to haunt us more subtly, as it suppresses our immune system and manifests in back and joint pain and diseases occurring in target organs symbolically corresponding to our rage.

According to Chinese herbal medicine, the liver is where anger and resentment is stored. Being the largest organ in the body, one of the functions of the liver is to detoxify pollutants and foreign materials the body does not need. A person with a toxic liver often turns yellow or bilious (excess bile). Someone whose liver is out of balance appears red and fiery, does not handle heat well, and becomes angry quite readily even though the anger often is not expressed. Anger, to the Chinese, is a toxic or an excessive emotion resulting from too much fire and needs purifying. Therefore, in order to be of sound mind and sound body and in equilibrium, we must confront our rage instead of allowing it to distract us with bodily symptoms of aches and pains as we suppress our feelings.

**Exhale Your Anger:** To face anger is to objectify it. We

should look at it like an impartial observer instead of a participant. This is extremely difficult to do during the heat of the moment. Breathing exercises help to oxygenate the brain to restore clarity and relax the heart. Instead of just counting to ten, practice taking ten breaths through the nose by inhaling to the count of two and exhaling to the count of four, that way we exhale more toxins and negativity than we inhale. Think about relaxing the heart while inhaling and exhaling.

**Identify What Really Hurts:** Pay attention to what body part is afflicted by our rage. For example, does our head, back, neck or stomach hurt? Each organ provides a clue to what we are feeling and why. Do I feel unsupported in my back or am I inflexible in my neck? Does my stomach hurt because I feel as if my solar plexus (representing the ego) has been attacked?

We should also not let anyone guilt or shame us because we have become angry; that often means they are afraid of anger (theirs and others). Emotions serve a purpose, even the more negative ones. They can be tools that help us learn, cope, grow and heal. Anger is no exception. It is powerful and healing to acknowledge our anger, step back for a moment, then decide what boundary has been crossed (if it is not obvious), and what needs to be done to make us feel safe, restored, respected, or at the very least validated.

When someone makes you angry, you are the only one that can control how it affects you and you alone. The other person will move on and forget. If you hold a grudge or let the anger fester inside you, it will only make you crazy.

Take some time to stop and think about what causes the anger inside you. Then work to avoid getting to that point at all costs. Sometimes it takes leaving a situation altogether, but at least you stay in control. Time is the key. Time to come to grips with your emotions. There is always a brief, sometimes very brief, moment before the explosion. Learn to recognise it and then control it.

## Meditation: Releasing Fears with the Consuming Eye of Ra

After centring yourself, bring your attention into the darkness that is before you. In this darkness, you see the eyes of Sekhmet, the Egyptian lioness goddess, gleaming back at you. As you inhale and exhale, the goddess appears standing before you as a woman's body with the head of a lioness, on top of which is the uraeus crown holding the sun disk. As "She who comes in Times of Chaos", Sekhmet takes offerings of fear, rage and weakness, and transforms them into alchemical gold, the universal medicine for physical, emotional and deep soul healing.

With each inhalation, allow yourself to connect with the goddess, eye to eye and heart to heart. Sekhmet may place her hand paw upon your chest where your anahata (or heart centre) is. Allow yourself to be open and feel her sekhem, her power, moving into your heart and then through your circulatory system into every cell of your being, filling you with her power.

As you continue to feel her power coursing through your being, Sekhmet begins to transform into her full lioness form. As she changes, so do you, transforming into a lion or lioness just like the goddess standing before you. Become aware of your breath, your newly transformed body and your muscles as they change. Feel whiskers grow and begin to sense how they communicate information to you. As you continue to inhale and exhale, stretch into the fullness of your lion or lioness being and follow Sekhmet, bounding across the African savanna.

Off in the distance you perceive the first fear coming to meet you. Sekhmet shows you how to stop and crouch in the grass to watch. Following what the goddess does, observe this fear closely. Listen carefully and sniff the air. You can smell it, maybe even taste it on your tongue. Notice when you feel the fear in your body and how your body reacts to it. Then ask yourself: "Is this fear something that still serves me?" If it does, honour it and thank it. If not, then transform the fear with Sekhmet's help by looking directly at the fear. As you do, you hear a low grumbling sound coming from deep inside of you. Allow the sound to build and then let it loose with a large roar. Take note as to how the fear reacts. Remember Sekhmet is right there with you. As the roar begins to diminish, so does the fear.

Continue hunting more of these fears in the African savanna, following the same process. As you seek out each fear, remember to honour and thank it, and then then let it go if it no longer serves you.

When there are no more fears showing up, walk side by side with Sekhmet, enjoying the sun in the aftermath of the hunt. With each step you take, slowly return to your human form, with Sekhmet returning to her goddess form. Bring your awareness back to your breath, and as you inhale and exhale, slowly return to the here and now, bringing your awareness to your physical body. When you are ready, gently move your fingers and toes, and then open your eyes.

# Lilith: The Original Wild Woman

*I am Lilith*
*Not to be controlled*
*I live in the wild with birds and the beasts and serpents of the desert*
*Call on me in lust.*

*I am Lilith*
*Demon woman, lover, murderess*
*I fly in the dark of night to steal your children, lie with your men*
*Call on me with dread.*

*I am Lilith*
*Irresistible, irredeemable*
*I have been the consort of Adam, of Samuel and of God*
*Call on me for power.*[38]

The inclusion of Lilith in any goddess work can be somewhat controversial simply for the fact that historically, she was never actually depicted as a goddess despite what some modern goddess-centric writers may portray. She was a demoness who had no ancient practices associated with her except that there were rites and amulets, often in the shape of knives that were constructed in order to protect the wearer from her and her demonic offspring. Nowhere in the Old Testament was Lilith recorded as being part of the Biblical creation myth, nor was she actually present in the original story of Adam and Eve. In fact, Lilith is mentioned only once, within the "Book of Isaiah" (34:14, *King James Bible*), relating to the vengeance of Yahweh:

"The wild shall meet with the jackal
And the Satyr shall cry to its fellow
And Lilith shall repose there and find her a place of rest".

The first medieval source believed to depict Adam and Lilith in full was the *Midrash Abkir* (ca. 10th century), which was followed by the Zohar and Kabbalistic writings, including the *Alphabet of Ben Sira*. In the *Midrash Abkir* Adam was described as being perfect until he recognized either his sin or Cain's homicide as being the cause of bringing death into the world. This realisation caused him to separate from Eve and fast for some 130 years. It is during this period of fasting that Lilith, also known as *Pizna* or *Naamah*, desired his beauty and came to him against his will. She bore him many demons and spirits called "the plagues of humankind".[39]

The *Alphabet of Ben Sira*[40], however, recorded Lilith as being Adam's first wife. As they were both created equal from dust she queried why she should lie beneath Adam during intercourse. When Adam insisted on the superior position, Lilith uttered the sacred name of God and flew away to the Red Sea (considered to be a place of ill-repute and populated by demons). Here she engaged in "unbridled promiscuity" and bore a brood of more than one hundred demons per day.

God sent three "enforcer" angels after her, being Senoy, Sansenoy and Semangelof, all of whom demanded she returned to Adam. After she refused, Lilith was advised that one hundred of her demon children would be slain every day until she did what was demanded of her. In response, Lilith stated she was created to cause sickness in infants, and that for male infants she had power over them until the eighth day (the day of the circumcision) and until the 20th day for female infants. The only time she would lose her power over an infant was if she saw an image or amulet bearing the names of the angels, and in such circumstances only then would she agree to one hundred of her own children perishing daily. This is a role that Lilith will continue to do until the Messiah returns and removes the "spirit of impurity".[41]

Bowls dating back to the 6th century CE have been found at the site of a Jewish settlement in Nippur, Babylon (modern day Iraq) that bear inscriptions mentioning Lilith. Here she was regarded as a "ghostly paramour of men and constituted a special danger to women during certain times of their sexual life cycle - before defloration and during menstruation".[42] Mothers and new born babies were considered to be especially vulnerable to Lilith's power and needed protection from her. A drawing on one of these bowls showed Lilith naked, with long loose hair, pointed breasts, strongly marked genitals and chained ankles. This image did not have wings like the Babylonian terracotta relief of a winged, owl-footed woman that is often interpreted as being Lilith which can be seen at the British museum.

Lilith's history, however, pre-dates Christianity. According to Swiss psychoanalyst and writer on Jewish mysticism, Siegmund Hurwitz[43], she first appeared around 4,000 BCE as a Sumerian group of wind and storm demons or spirits that were collectively referred to as the "Lilitu". The Sumerians also recorded a succubus creature known as the "Ardat Lili" (where *Ardatu* was a term that described a young woman of marrying age and *lili* being a type of demon) who was credited with "night-hag syndrome"[44]. This creature was also said to cause erotic dreams, thus robbing a man of semen and spiritual vitality. This could indicate the connection with a further Sumerian word "lulu", a word meaning "wantonness", which may have shaped our modern interpretation of Lilith.

Amongst the Sumerian king list, the name *Lilu* was listed as the hero Gilgamesh's father who functioned as an incubus, or a male demon, disturbing women during their sleep, in order to have sexual intercourse with them. Further, within Mesopotamian mythology can be found the *Lamashtu*, a female demon that menaced women during childbirth and kidnapped breastfeeding infants in order to gnaw their bones and suck their blood. This demi-goddess was said to be the daughter of the sky god Anu, and incantations against her referred to her as being a malevolent yet free willed daughter of heaven who exercised her free will over infants, seduced men, drank blood and caused disease, sickness and death.[45]

In Assyrian text, there was a demon "lilitu" who preyed upon women and children, and who was described as being associated with lions, storms, desert and disease. Early portrayals of these demons which dwelt in desolate and desert places, depicting them as having bird talons for feet and wings (reflecting the "Lilith" Babylonian relief as mentioned earlier). They were also thought to have been highly sexually predatory towards men, but were not able to copulate normally.

As *Lilitu*, Lilith was also considered to be a sacred prostitute[46] to the Babylonian goddess Ishtar where she performed sexual acts in the context of religious worship. Hurwitz made similar claims with respect to her being a "hand maiden" to the Sumerian goddess Inanna whereby, according to an ancient Sumerian myth "Inanna and the Huluppu Tree": "Inanna has sent the beautiful, unmarried, and seductive prostitute Lilitu out into the fields and streets in order to lead men astray"[47]. Here, Lilitu also had the power to kill any living plant she touched and due to her beauty and fluidity of movement, this made her irresistible and therefore alluding to Lilith, with her snake-like connections, as being deceptive and manipulative. Little evidence, however, can be found to Hurwitz's claims, likewise the claim that she dwelt in the trunk of the Huluppu tree which was later cut down to make a throne for Inanna.

Lilith's beauty and reputation of being perceived as the first femme fatale of human history was depicted in the rather controversial painting by John Collier (1850-1934) where she is shown as a "beautiful maiden" standing in a slightly erotic pose with a giant boa constrictor wrapping itself around her naked body. Lilith has an expression of ecstasy on her face. Her white naked body stands out as the darker snake tends to blend in with darkened woods behind her.

## Working with Lilith

Regardless of history, Lilith, demon or deity, does present a powerful message that we can use today. For women, she represents independence (she bowed down to no man, not Adam, and not even Yahweh) and has become a symbol of feminine power, especially through sexuality. With respect to sexuality, this is for pleasure itself as she is not associated with fertility. The children she "destroys" can be linked to a woman's menstrual cycle, the failure of a man's semen to impregnate. This specifically connects Lilith with the sacred blood mysteries, and the act of women understanding their own ovulation cycle in order to engage in sexual intercourse without necessarily becoming pregnant.

Often though, Lilith represents that part of our subconscious which is most animal like – defiant, uncivilised, passionate and basically natural, especially when it comes to sex and sexuality. While this may sound appealing, as a succubus nature, it can drain us of our vitality, turning us into a "thoughtless animal". Lilith's demonic off-spring may also represent our own personal demons, the imbalances of our mind that can lead to neurosis and even our own destruction. This is what enables Lilith to be included as a Dark Goddess.

What is often overlooked in the modern interpretations of Lilith is, whilst there is an attraction to her dark beauty, we still need to approach her with an element of care. She represents the darker side of the feminine psyche where, as a "Mother of the Night", she opens the doorways to the realms of hidden pleasures, enticing us to step through. If we do not have the ability to balance her temptations with cultural understanding of woman's place in human society there is a real danger of getting lost in this realm, which always comes at a great personal cost.

The sexual aspect of Lilith can be an extremely complicated issue for women today, especially those who have been brought up where there have been rules or expectations governing our sexuality. As we move from childhood to young adulthood, we may find ourselves torn between the desire to be wanted and the obligation to "save our self" (i.e., our maidenhood) for someone special. Ironically our Western culture surrounds us with mixed attitudes about a young woman's sexuality. If we "save our self" and become the "good girl", we are seen as a loser, frigid, a tease, or worse, that no one wants us because we are unattractive and unwanted. Yet our sexuality, especially our maidenhood, is so highly prized that it can be used as a bartering tool, sometimes by other people without our full knowledge or even consent. We may even find that once our maidenhood has been offered up, when we have sex we become tarnished, stained, untouchable and worse a "dirty" girl. It is these labels that can haunt us throughout our adult life and affect how we embrace our sexuality and more importantly our sensuality.

When we work with Lilith, she can often bring about an aspect of the divined feminine quite unfamiliar to us, that of the vicarious sexual partner. It is Lilith who reminds men that sex is an act between two people and not just a solo action, therefore consideration needs to be shown towards their partner. Lilith also challenges men on how they perceive women, reminding them that a woman should not be justified or labelled, that there is more to the opposite sex/gender, and when treated with respect, the female is just as dynamic as the male. The feminine aspect is not always physical. As Jung pointed out, we all have both an anima and animus side to our personalities.

According to Demeter George[48], Lilith can also be seen as a threefold archetype, in that at first she shows us how and where we experience suppression, resentment and explosive anger, as well as when we have taken a stand for our dignity, only to be rejected and are forced to flee. Lilith then brings us to the exile of desolation where we feel our anguish, alienation, fear and hatred for our own sexuality. Finally, we can discover the on the apple itself, this piece of fruit that has been connected with temptation, seduction and even the downfall of human kind. What does temptation mean to you? How does it play a part in your life? Do you give in to temptation easily, or hold yourself back? How do you feel when you allow yourself to be tempted?

As you continue to slowly devour the apple your thoughts begin to focus on your opinions of sensuality and sexuality. What do these mean to you? Where did these opinions originate? How do you feel about these thoughts? What do they mean to you today? What does sexuality mean? What does sensuality mean? Do they play a part in your life today? In your thoughts? Those thoughts about yourself? About your partner (past or present)? Your relationships?

Do you shy away from sensuality, thinking or talking about it? Or are you open about discussing it? What about sexuality? How do you view this? Do you consider sensuality and sexuality to be the same or similar?

When was the last time you felt sensual or sexual? Do you need someone else to make you feel sensual or sexual, or are you able to make your self feel this way? How do you relate to your sexuality? Do you have any boundaries? How do other people relate to your sexuality? How do you relate to the sexuality demonstrated by other people?

As you continue to eat the apple, allow the answers to these questions flow in and out of your thoughts, providing you with insight as to where they came from and whether they are still relevant for you today. Any thoughts that do not serve you, or you feel are irrelevant, visualise them being released from you like early morning mist dissipating from a pond.

When you have finished eating the apple and focusing on your opinions about sensuality and sexuality, bring your attention back to your breathing. Before you, the leaves of the Tree of Life gently rustle in the breeze that refreshes your soul. You notice

# The Gorgon Medusa

*Medusa once had charms; to gain her love.*
*A rival crowd of envious lovers strove.*
*They, who have seen her, own, they ne'er did trace*
*More moving features in a sweeter face.*
*Yet above all, her length of hair, they own,*
*In golden ringlets wav'd, and graceful shone.*[49]

Medusa is commonly known as the snake-haired monster who would turn anyone who looked at her into stone. Far from being a divine goddess, this popular image of Medusa stems from the Greek poet Hesiod's *Theogony* (written sometime between the 8th and 7th century BCE) where she is only briefly mentioned as one of three sisters "grey from their birth" who were referred to as the Graeae, the Gorgons, whose father was Phorcys ("Old Man of the Sea") and Ceto (a female sea monster). The Graeae were said to have lived just beyond the edges of the earth where the sun and the moon are unable to reach, and their names were Stheno ("might"), Euryale ("wide flowing sea") and Medusa ("Queen")[50]. Of her sisters it was Medusa who "suffered a woeful fate" because she was born mortal, and her death was caused by the hero Perseus who cut off her head.[51] Hesiod excludes from mentioning why Perseus cut off Medusa's head or what he did with it afterwards.

Vase painters from the 5th century BCE envisaged the Gorgons as both monstrous and beautiful. In the 5th century BCE another Greek poet, Pindar, described Medusa as being "fair cheeked" and even "beautiful" in his *Pythian 12*. Today we are familiar with Medusa being the stuff of nightmares with her hideous swollen face framed by hissing snakes, bulging eyes, tusks of a boar, and protruding tongue. It is little wonder she has the ability to turn mortals to stone with only one glance.

The back story as to why Medusa is the only Gorgon sister who had snakes for hair can be found in Book IV of the Roman poet Ovid's *The Metamorphoses*, thought to have been written in the 7th century CE. Here we learn that she was once an extremely beautiful maiden and possible devotee (or even priestess) at a temple dedicated to Minerva (the Roman equivalent to Athena). Her hair was one of her most outstanding features. Medusa's beauty drew many suitors, one of which was the Roman God of the Oceans, Neptune (Poseidon to the Greeks), who "violated" (raped) her in the temple. Despite being a victim, Medusa was the one who received the outrage of Minerva (Athena to the Greeks). Using her deific ability, Minerva/Athena turned Medusa's beautiful hair into snakes that would terrify any man who came near her, and also cursed her so that her gaze would turn them into stone.

In Apollodorus of Athens' *Bibliotheke*[52] (written around the 1st century BCE), Polydectes, the King of Seriphos, secretly wanted to marry Perseus's mother, Danae, however, Perseus was preventing this, so Polydectes pretended he was collecting horses as a wedding gift for the Princess Hippodamia. As Perseus was not wealthy, he told the king that as he had no horse to give, he would secure any other thing Polydectes wanted as a gift. The king asked for the Gorgon Medusa's head, secretly believing Perseus would fail in the task and be turned to stone.

Perseus, however, became aware of the plot and being half divine (his father was said to be Zeus), enlisted assistance from the other gods. Athena gave him a highly polished shield and instructed Perseus where to find the Hesperides, who were known as the "Daughters of the Evening". They gave him a *kibisis* (bag) into which he was to put Medusa's head. The hero then acquired the Sword of Adamantine and Hades' helm (a cap of invisibility) from Zeus, and finally, Hermes lent him his winged sandals.

Once armed with these weapons Perseus was able to locate

the cave in which Medusa was residing. He used the shield to guide him and behead her. As he did this, a winged horse known as the Pegasus sprung from her neck. Perseus took the head to Polydectes which petrified everyone present when it was revealed from the knapsack. Athena later placed Medusa's head upon her shield.

These differing versions of Medusa's story tend to lead to the assumption that there may have been even still more to the myth than what we are familiar with today. While Kottke believes Medusa's name means "queen", from an etymological perspective it is derived from the ancient Greek *medo* meaning "to guard or protect"[53]. Feminist writers such as Patricia Monaghan[54] believe that Medusa's name means "sovereign female wisdom" as it allegedly stems from the same Indo-European root as the Sanskrit *Medha* and the Greek *Metis*, meaning "wisdom" and "intelligence".

Another feminist author, Laura Shannon[55], is of the opinion that Medusa was originally a Libyan goddess who was worshipped by the Amazons as their serpent goddess. Medusa (Metis who was a Titan goddess prior to the reign of the Olympians) was also believed to have been the destroyer aspect of a triple goddess who were also called Neith, Anath, Athene or Ath-enna in North Africa and Athana in 1,400 BCE Minoan Crete. This makes her an aspect of Athena.

If Shannon is correct, then Medusa may have risen from the primeval floodwaters, as did both Neith and Anath before her. In classic Greek mythology Lake Tritonis in Libya was named after a goddess-nymph of the same name, and was considered to be the birth place of the triple moon goddess where Athena represented the Maiden, Metis the Mother, and Medusa represented, the Crone aspects. Ancient inscriptions about the North African moon goddess describe Medusa as:

"I have come from myself. I am all that has been and that will be, and no mortal has yet been able to lift the veil that covers me."

There is further thought that Medusa's head was, in fact, a mask that initiated priestesses used to wear during specific sacred rites and rituals in order to frighten off those attendees who had not reached the level of awareness needed to sufficiently understand such rites and rituals. According to Jamie Walters, these masks also symbolized the initiates' own level of knowing, the gnosis, and that the snakes on the masks were symbolic of the cycle of life, transformation and the deeper mysteries.[56]

Walters claims that Medusa's name may have actually meant "sovereign feminine wisdom" and when she was slain by Perseus it was due to a possible rise against this feminine power. This thought seems to echo what Robert Graves[57] suggested in that the myth of Perseus preserved the memory of conflicts that occurred between the sexes in the transition from matriarchal to patriarchal societies around the Mediterranean. The decapitation of Medusa is therefore the patriarchal answer to the existence of women's full powers, to decapitate them into silence.

Amulets bearing grotesque faces resembling what has been termed as "Gorgoneion" (i.e., a female head with opened mouth and snake-like hair) have been used to ward off evil and malign influences since the 8th century BCE in ancient Greece[58]. It is the use of such images that may have led Kottke to assert that the Gorgoneion mask of Medusa had been entwined with history where it represented death as well as fear.[59] Kottke is of the view that the ancient Greeks believed there were three different beings making up the different qualities of death. The only male of the trio was Thanatos, who is the least frightful aspect, as he was equated with the taking of the heroes who died in battle, so was perceived with honour as opposed to fear. The other two beings associated with death were female, Ker and Gorgo, who were equally feared as they represented the loss of control that men had when death called for them. According to Kottke this perception was carried over to the image of the Gorgons and the way they have been viewed in mythology.

## Working with Medusa

Medusa's widely recognised symbol of female wisdom was her threatening, ceremonial mask, which has wide unblinking eyes that reflect her immense wisdom. They are all knowing, all seeing eyes that see through us, penetrating our illusions and looking into the abyss of truth. Her mouth is deathly; it looks like a skull. It is devouring of all life, returning us to the source. Her tongue protrudes like that of a snake and her face is surrounded by a halo of spiralling, serpentine hair that symbolises the great cycles and her serpent wisdom.

As a Dark Goddess, Medusa rips away our mortal illusions. She represents the forbidden yet liberating wisdom and the untameable forces of nature. As a young and beautiful woman, she is fertility and life, whilst as a Crone Goddess she consumes by devouring all on the earth plane. Through death we must return to the source, the abyss of transformation, the timeless realm. We must yield to her and her terms of mortality. She reflects a culture in harmony with nature.

Medusa is also considered to represent the collective fury that women have experienced for many, many centuries due to repression. As Shannon points out, her fearsome face is framed with snakes and she has the ability to paralyse with a glance making Medusa terrifying, yet when we take a closer look, she is also the one who is terrified. All the images of her depict the frozen expression of an open-mouthed scream with eyes wide and teeth bared. For Shannon this "gut-wrenching image is an eloquent expression of women's rage", as well as trauma.[60]

Archetypal psychologist James Hillman states that myths live vividly in our symptoms. With this in mind, the three key elements found within Medusa's myth are rage (of Athena), paralysis

(Medusa's ability to turn people into stone) and disembodiment (how Perseus kills her), all of which are classic symptoms of post-traumatic stress disorder (more commonly referred to as PTSD). Shannon points out that, according to trauma healing expert Bessel van der Kolk, numbing, freezing, and immobilization are common responses to trauma, in particular sexual trauma. PTSD causes a sense of being emotionally shut down, and when long-term trauma is held within the body, this can result in stiff, rigid, or stilted movement, posture, and expression, all of which resemble paralysis. Trauma can erode key social skills of self-control and self-regulation, causing the uncontrollable rage characteristic of PTSD. The brutal separation of head from body, a third element of Medusa's story, may reflect dissociation, fragmentation, and disconnection from the body also typical of the post-traumatic state.

When we work with Medusa, we must resolve to be totally truthful with ourselves – to act from our inner core. This is because she can assist us to change our own consciousness, our perception of things. This can be daunting and difficult to accept, not to mention to embrace completely if the change appears to be contrary to how we were brought up, the way people around us (especially our loved ones) live their lives, and other daily influences. For those of us who seek a greater understanding of who we truly are, then Medusa is the perfect aspect of the Dark Goddess to help us identify who this person is that lives within our own skin.

## Invocation to Medusa

Hail to thee, Medusa
Great protector of women with snakes for hair
You who are numinous, the shapeshifter.
I call thee, Medusa.
Make your presence known within me
Release me from my frozen rage

Purge me from my denied truths
Enable me to embrace the darkness of my soul
Ornate Pulchra Goni! [I praise the beautiful Gorgon]
Ornate Pulchra Goni! [I praise the beautiful Gorgon]
Ornate Pulchra Goni! [I praise the beautiful Gorgon]

## Correspondences associated with Medusa

Snakes, serpents, hair, Pegasus, mirror, normal rocks (not crystals), caves, dark moon, red and black colours, frankincense, calendula, pine, dragon's blood resin, black onyx, quartz crystal, obsidian.

## Exercise: Discovering Medusa's Soul Mirror

This exercise has been adapted from the "Soul Mirror" taught by Austrian occultist Franz Bardon. To find out who we truly are, we need to be 100 per cent honest with ourselves when we undertake this exercise, as the only person we are cheating is our own self.

List all the positive attributes about yourself that you can think of on one page, and the negative ones on another other. When you have compiled your lists, the next step is to align them to one of the elements – fire, air, earth and water. The objective is to group both the negative as well as the positive attributes of your personality into elemental representations. Keep in mind, however, that some may overlap.

In doing this, you will be able to gain insight into aspects of your personality that you may not be aware of. You may discover what element you are most attuned with. You may like to compare your discoveries to your astrological natal chart. From here, elemental meditations and self-awareness are enacted to help balance a potential unbalanced individual. This exercise can form part of an ongoing guide for self-improvement, working on one attribute at a time.

## Changing Habits

The simplest way to do this is to use a rosary or mala (string of beads[61]) and recite positive self-affirmations twice a day (upon rising and prior to doing to bed as this is when you are in a very relaxed state of consciousness, making it easier to imprint these different affirmations into your subconscious mind). The use of positive self-affirmations will build up your willpower, but *you* are the one who has to make the change. This means you actually have to want to change, not secretly hope for someone or something else to do it for you.

Think about the current positive self-affirmations you are working with throughout the day. Just let them pop up as a reminder to avoid doing something or to act a certain way. This will further impregnate your subconscious mind with the intent for creating positive personality traits.[62]

# Morgan le Fay: A Transforming Illusion

*"No-one knows the real story of the great King Arthur of Camelot. Most of what you think you know about Camelot, Gwenhwyfar, Lancelot and the evil sorceress known as Morgaine le Fay, is nothing but lies. I should know, for I am Morgaine le Fay, priestess of the Isle of Avalon, where the ancient religion of the Mother Goddess was born."*

(Morgaine, *Mists of Avalon*, Turner Network Television, 2001)

A much-loved character within the modern telling of the Arthurian legend, thanks to *The Mists of Avalon*[63], Morgan le Fay appears to be a unique aspect of the Dark Goddess in that she battles with what are very human qualities, in particular self-identity and later self-worth. The following essay has been adapted from a longer essay that I wrote, which appears in *The Faerie Queens: A Collection of Essays Exploring the Myths, Magic and Mythology of the Faerie Queens* edited by Sorita d'Este (Avalonia, 2013)

The version of the Arthurian legend that we are familiar with today, of King Arthur and his band of knights including Lancelot, Queen Guinevere, and the sorceress Morgan le Fay stems from the *Le Morte d'Arthur* by Sir Thomas Malory which appeared in the late 15th century. Throughout the 21 books that make up what has been hailed as the greatest piece of English literature to have emerged from the Medieval era, Morgan le Fay appears largely to be the bane of her half-brother, King Arthur's, existence.

*Le Morte d'Arthur* commences with a meeting having taken place between Uther Pendragon, the King of Britain, and Gorlois, the Duke of Tintagel, who had been accompanied by his wife, the beautiful Igraine. When the king took a fancy to Igraine, Gorlois abruptly returned to Cornwall, placed his wife at Tintagel castle and proceeded to battle Uther, who took offence to the Duke's withdrawal from the meeting without his consent. It was during this battle that the king's advisor and magician, Merlin, used his magic to disguise Uther as the Duke, enabling him to slip into the castle and bed Igraine, which resulted in Arthur, the future king, being conceived. Gorlois subsequently lost his life in the battle, enabling Uther to marry Igraine. At this point in Malory's telling, Morgan is first briefly mentioned as being one of three sisters and was "put to school in a nunnery, and there she learned so much that she was a great clerk of necromancy."[64] She was later wedded to King Uriens of the land of Gore (part of modern day Cornwall).

Morgan and Arthur do not actually meet until towards the end of Book 1 when Igraine was summoned before the court to verify Arthur's bloodline, to which meeting she brings her daughter, Morgan le Fay.

In Book 2, Morgan's hatred towards Arthur started to show, although no clear reason was given as to why she harboured such emotions, only her attempts to kill him through the use of magic and enchantment. The first being that Arthur "betoke the scabbard of Excalibur to Morgan le Fay, his sister".[65] Why he does this is not explained, only her desire to pass the scabbard on to her lover Accolon: Her plot failed when Arthur and Accolon found themselves caught up in a feud between two brothers that resulted in Arthur killing Accolon, but not before the lover confessed his relationship with Morgan and that the reason behind the feuding brothers in the first place was her scheme to have Arthur placed in a position where he could be killed. Despite this, Arthur referred to Morgan as a "kind sister". That was until Morgan sent "the richest mantle that ever was seen in that court, for it was set as full of precious stones ... and there were the richest stones that ever the king saw"[66] to the court. When the Lady of the Lake intervened, it was revealed that the mantle was in fact laced with poison.

Morgan does not appear again until Book 9 when she attempted to expose the adulterous affair between Queen Guinevere and Sir Lancelot. After having her plans fail once again, Morgan basically disappeared from Malory's story until the final book where she was recorded as being one of three queens who received Arthur on the magical isle of Avalon after he received the fatal wound from his son Mordred at the battle of Camlann.

Malory alludes that Mordred's mother was the wife of King Lot of Orkney (mother of four sons, Gawaine, Gaheris, Agravine and Gareth, all of whom were knights of Arthur's Round Table). When Arthur lay with King Lot's wife, he was apparently unaware that she was in fact his sister, Margawse. In later adaptations, including John Boorman's 1981 movie "Excalibur" and Marion Zimmer Bradley's 1987 novel, *The Mists of Avalon*, Mordred's mother was Morgan. Boorman portrayed the liaison as part of a sinister plan Morgan (played by Helen Mirren) hatched in order to rule; whereas Bradley depicted it as being part of an ancient Beltaine fertility rite, where the "Virgin Huntress" (a role enacted by Morgan) coupled with the "Stag King" (unknowingly enacted by Arthur), and the child of that union is considered sacred.

Malory's interpretation of Morgan le Fay within the Arthurian legend appears to have gone through a number of transformations since it first briefly appeared in *Vita Merlini* (also known as *The Life of Merlin*) written by Geoffrey of Monmouth in c.1150 CE. Here, Morgan barely got a mention save that she was one of nine sisters who dwelt on the magical island located in the sea which was referred to as the island of apples, or "the Fortunate Isle", Avalon. She was renowned for her knowledge of healing through the use of herbs, her beauty and her ability to shapeshift.

Morgan continued being described as being one of great beauty with magical healing powers up until the 13th century with the publication of a collection of prose known as the Vulgate Cycle, which was believed to have formed the basis to Malory's *Le Morte d'Arthur*. The longest prose within the Vulgate Cycle is the "Lancelot Propre" (Lancelot Proper), where Morgan was given human characteristics by being described as the youngest daughter of Gorlois, the Duke of Cornwall, and the Lady Igraine as opposed to some enchanted healer. The Vulgate Cycle also placed Morgan in a castle as opposed to Avalon, and her use of her magical powers was for manipulative or evil purposes, as opposed to healing.

From her first appearance in *Vita Merlini* ("The Life of Merlin"), Morgan's personal power and innate magical abilities wane as she is transformed from a "loving fairy with the ability to heal" to a schizophrenic and disenchanted woman in *Le Morte d'Arthur*. By the time of Malory, the skills Morgan possessed were taught to her by Merlin, and were largely used to preserve her youthful appearance, or to seek revenge.

Despite an attempt to humanise Morgan, her Otherworldly or fairy connections continue through until modern day. This may be because of the origins of her name as Lynne Sinclair-Wood[67] suggests that Morgan, meaning "women (or woman) of the sea" and may have originally referred to a title as opposed to an actual name." Leila Norako[68] agrees with this suggestion by indicating that Morgan may have originated from Brittany, as local folklore contains fairy sprites, the "mari-morgan". Folklorist W.Y. Evan-Wentz[69] offers a different origin and describes "the Île Molène" (the Morgan) as "a fairy eternally young, a virgin seductress whose passion, never satisfied, drives her to despair".

Arthurian expert, John Mathews, perceives Morgan as a "tutelary spirit" or a goddess of Avalon, the Otherworld, and that her animosity towards Arthur is an aspect of the challenging and testing role that such figures eternally offer in order to discover who among their followers is actually worthy of favour.[70] This point seems to be strengthened by the 14th century tale of "Gawain and the Green Knight", where Morgan tests warriors for their courage. He further asserts that as Morgan has become "... known by the epithet 'le Fay' (the fairy)" this means she managed to retain many of her original goddess qualities which could explain the reasoning why, despite the animosity she allegedly depicted towards her brother, Morgan took Arthur to Avalon when he was dying.

In Zimmer Bradley's *The Mists of Avalon* Morgaine (as Morgan was called), was described as being "a fairy child, one of the fellows of the hallow hills"[71] by her father, Gorlois, prior to her fostering on Avalon where her aunt, Viviane, ruled as Lady of the Lake. This fairy reference continues throughout the book, resulting with Viviane, the Lady of the Lake, advising that Morgaine bears the royal blood line of the "Old People", and that:

> "...in the ancient days long before the wisdom and the religion of the Druids came here from the sunken temples in the western continent, the fairy people, of who we are both born, you and I my Morgaine, lived here on the shores of the inland sea..."[72] (which is Avalon).

In her dissertation of Morgan within *Le Morte d'Arthur*, Mary Lynn Soul brings to our attention the fact that from the outset of the myth, Morgan does not appear to fit the characteristics and mannerisms of the "conventionally passive woman" of the Middle Ages, in that she kidnaps Lancelot, orders knights to pursue or destroy Lancelot or Tristram, attempts to expose the adultery of Guinevere ...".[73] Morgan is also portrayed as a woman of control in that she has her own castle that she can defend and spares no mercy for her husband. Instead of being subservient and demure, blending totally into the background, it is her rebellious nature that comes to light, right from her initial recorded action where she manipulates a battle between her lover Accolon and Arthur in order to rule the country herself. Soul therefore suggests that the depiction of Morgan could possibly be an expression of masculine fear of a woman's power when she is not controlled by any man. It is interesting to note that at the time of Malory, there were increasing restrictions on women healers such as Morgan, and, when coupled with her rebellion against the social norms of the time, this would have cast her under great suspicion as being perceived as a witch.

In *The Mists of Avalon*, Morgaine's goal appears not to be to usurp Arthur from his throne, but to bring people back to the worship of the goddess as opposed to the new religion of Christianity. She is still depicted as a flawed character, in particular in her inability to find happiness and peace. This, however, does not appear to prevent Morgan being ironically described today as "a role model for women (and men) who wish to 'take their power' in this world"[74]. It is also interesting to note that despite the malicious or confused depiction of Morgan, modern writers such as Kathy Jones refer to her being "... a great healer who can heal us of our deepest wounds"[75]. Jones also describes Morgan as the "mother of time and space, the weaver of the web, of the matrix of life itself"[76]. This is interesting, considering Morgan's disassociation with life and her unacceptance of her role of Lady of the Lake and High Priestess of Avalon, as depicted in *The Mists of Avalon*, as well as how she is portrayed in other interpretations, including Malory's *Le Morte d'Arthur*.

## Working with Morgan le Fay

As shown with each evolution of the Arthurian legend, Morgan tends to have moved further and further away from her original fae-like character and associations. Even in *The Mists of Avalon*, save for the island of Avalon being Otherworldly, Morgan appears far from her original faery-like roots. Yet despite this modern depiction, Morgan is still referred to as being inspirational to women by feminist writers, and within the goddess spiritual movement. Maybe it is her somewhat flawed character, filled with contradictions, that draws many of us to her. In Morgan we identify our own selves as we are often encouraged to present ourselves in a certain way in order to meet external expectations, as opposed to listening and following what our heart (or deeper soul) desires. It is this perception of Morgan that qualifies her inclusion as a Dark Goddess.

## Invocation to Morgan le Fay

Come, o come, Morgan of the fae
Queen of the faeries, keeper of the Old Ways
Through your pain, I feel life
Through your confusion, I see purpose
Through your denial, I embrace all possibilities
Shapeshifter, healer, beloved of all secrets
Spin your sacred web around me.
Reveal to me the ancient knowledge
Come, o come, Queen of the Faeries,
Morgan le Fay.

## Correspondences associated with Morgan le Fay

Apples, fairies, scrying, ravens, crows, dark of the moon, lakes, purple and black colours, clear quartz, amethyst, black onyx, blue goldstone, swords, rosemary, frankincense, eucalyptus, marjoram.

## Exercise: Embracing Your True Self

Greek philosopher Aristotle said: "Knowing yourself is the beginning of all wisdom." Just like Morgan le Fay did, it is easy for us to forget that one of our purposes in this life is to take full and honest responsibility in understanding our own selves, including behavioural patterns. The following five steps are designed to assist you in knowing yourself.

**Familiar with Your Mind:** Take the time to witness without reacting to your thoughts, feelings, sensations, and the images that arise in your mind. Mastering the practice of detachment does take time, however, even by taking small steps, benefits can quickly be noticed. If you are feeling anxious, for example, rather than becoming attached to the feeling, try and observe what is going on in your mind and choose not to get caught up in it.

**Familiar with Your Younger Self:** Before you let go of your past self, find out whether there are any unresolved issues that need to be addressed or even acknowledged. If your younger self grew up in a chaotic environment, then as a consequence you may have made some lifestyle choices during your teenage years that you may still feel ashamed of today. Find an old photograph of yourself from your childhood and ask that child what wisdom do they have to show you. What is revealed may very well surprise you.

**Acknowledge Grief:** We often spend most of our time avoiding grief. However, if we never take the time to feel this emotion, it can accumulate. Note how actions in our lives could warrant the feelings of grief as outlined earlier. The shedding of tears and learning how to release grief enables us to clear out any staleness in our anahata (heart) chakra, and in doing so, enables us to heal any wounds we have not attended to. Once the grief is felt and the clearing allowed, joy can enter our lives and we are able to explore the self on a deeper level.

**Being Direct with Your Ego:** This means getting to know your true self and being willing to face the truth through the understanding of your faults. If we are worried about what people think of us, then we can never truly be our authentic self around them. We all have a past that makes us the person we are today. However, it is important to find the courage to understand the parts of yourself that prevent you from moving forward. Record these parts without judgment or shame and welcome these facets of yourself with compassion and patience.

**Build Honest Relationships:** While having the compassion and support of another, whether it is a good friend, spiritual teacher or even a therapist, can valuable, the most important person to be honest with is your own self. If you are not available to be completely honest with yourself then how can you be completely honest with other people?

## Meditation: Past Life Exploration with Morgan le Fay

Begin by sitting in a comfortable position, with your spine straight and eyes closed. Take a couple of slow deep breaths, breathing into your diaphragm, and releasing slowly. As you continue to breathe deeply, exhale as if you are a fire-breathing dragon, exhaling flames of tension. Inhale deeply, and slowly exhale, seeing how far your flames of tension will extend. Continue this deep breathing pattern for a few more times until you feel your physical body starting to relax.

Imagine you are standing on a small wooden jetty on the bank of a lake surrounded by forests. The water is calm and tranquil. The lake is so wide you are not able to see the other edge, however, in the distance across the lake you notice the outline of a barge or a flat boat slowly coming towards you. It is being punted by a hooded figure. The barge arrives at the jetty and the hooded figures assists you as you step onto the barge. This motion causes the barge to rock gently back and forth, back and forth, and as you are rocking, you sense you are starting to enter a state of relaxation. It feels so comfortable to be gently rocked by the boat as the barge is pushed off from the jetty and you are carried effortlessly across the water.

A bank of mist begins to descend, and you can feel its dampness on your skin. You close your eyes as this dampness brings back fond memories of an earlier time, a more peaceful time. As you open your eyes again, you see the mist parting again, just like a curtain, allowing entry into another realm, a world beyond the mist. Here is a land bathed in sunlight, and you see a familiar village on the foreshore, behind which is a mountain peak. As a light breeze plays with your hair, you smile to yourself. This is Avalon, and you have come home.

As you alight from the barge you are greeted by an older woman with long dark hair cascading down her back. She has a blue tattoo of a crescent moon high on her forehead that is now faded with age. She introduces herself to you, she is Morgan le Fay, and she has been waiting a long time for you to return to Avalon.

Taking you by the hand, Morgan le Fay leads you through the village, acknowledging some of the people as you pass who are going about their daily chores of tending to the abundant gardens, spinning and weaving wool, making crafts and herbal potions, and preparing foodstuffs. As you walk with Morgan still gently holding your hand, you take in the scents and sounds around you, the gentle chatter in the distance, bird calls, and the aroma of apples. As you focus ahead of you, you notice you have started to climb the mountain, moving through a grove of apple trees, in the middle of which is a stone well.

Stopping before the well, Morgan le Fay tells you that the water in the well is not used for drinking but for scrying. She asks if you would like to look in to the inky blackness of the well water and journey to a point in your past that still has an influence on your current life. You indicate that you do and she moves her hands over the top of the well, chanting an incantation before motioning to you to step closer. As you look down, the surface of the well water begins to ripple. Morgan le Fay tells you to continue to watch the water, and as you do, the surface begins to still, allowing you to gaze beyond it into the inky blackness below onto which images that provide insight to your query start to form.

When the images finally disappear and the well water is still, you know that your scrying session has ended. You thank Morgan le Fay for the opportunity and insight that you have received. In return she asks that you make an offering. For the first time you notice that you are wearing a belt from which a small leather bag is hanging. Reaching inside the bag you draw out a clear stone similar to a piece of quartz. Morgan le Fay smiles and motions towards the well. You drop the stone into the well as your offering. Then you are escorted back to down the path, through the village to the jetty where your barge is waiting for you.

You climb aboard the barge again and as it gently punts off, Morgan le Fay is waving farewell to you, along with some of the people you had passed on your way to the well. The mists descend again as the gentle rocking of the boat soothes you. When the mists dissipate, you see the forests where you began your journey. You are returning, feeling clear and centred, feeling you know what you need to do: returning, feeling refreshed and revitalized.

As you alight from the barge, you become more and more aware of your breathing. You take a deep breath and release it slowly, coming fully back into your body. Take another deep breath and, as you release it, open your eyes.

# Kali: The Hindu Dark Mother

*There is no light, not any motion*
*There is no mass, or nay sound*
*Still, in the lampless heart of the ocean*
*Fasten me down and hold me drowned*
*Within thy womb, within thy thought*
*Where there is naught*
*Where there is naught.*[77]

Kali is one of the more mysterious and enigmatic of the Hindu goddesses, and even to the Westerner, she brings about feelings of awesomeness (albeit often greatly misunderstood). She holds the energies of life and death and is similar to the Greek Fates or the Norse Norns, only that she is all of them rolled into one.

Shambhavi Chopra indicated that Kali's "Vedic roots depict her as a fire goddess of the dark blue light of the sun that is reflected in the dark pupil of the eye and its ability to see"[78]. This makes Kali a goddess of infinite space and eternal time.

Her appearance has generated a considerable amount of fear and misunderstanding. Having black or blue skin, with wild hair, Kali is often depicted in an aggressive manner, wearing a skirt made from severed hands and dancing on the corpse of her consort, Shiva. With her red tongue hanging down upon her chin, dripping with blood, it is little wonder the British colonists considered her to be an embodiment of evil. This, however, could not be further from the truth.

Her nakedness represents truth that is devoid of any pretence, with her long black unbound hair representing unbounded freedom and absolute truth. The hairpiece or crown on top of her head represents careful control, as all freedom carries a degree of responsibility (or the ability to respond to both our internal and external environment).

In her hands[79] she holds a *trishul* (trident) which represents the three *gunas* (energies of nature), the severed head (signifying the demise of ignorance and the ego), a bowl or skull cup *(kapala)* that is used to catch the blood from severed heads (blood being the essence of life), and a *scimitar*, a sword with a curved blade that represents divine knowledge which slays the ego in order for the state of *Mohska* (liberation from *samsara*, the constant cycle of birth, death and rebirth of the soul) to be attained. In some images one hand is downward in the *varada* (blessing) mudra indicating that those worshiping her with a true heart will be saved by her, and some images also have her displaying the upright *abhaya* (fearless) mudra or hand gesture. From her ears, Kali wears the heads of slain demons as earrings, and around her neck is a necklace containing 54 skulls, all of which are smiling due to being liberated from the constraints of the ego. Within the Hindu Tantric tradition, it is believed that the whole universe is but an expression of the primordial sound (vibration) which is represented by the Sanskrit alphabet. Being an embodiment of this sacred alphabet, each of the skulls that Kali wears around her neck represents a Sanskrit seed sound.

As a goddess of destruction, Kali is also one of purification, in that what is destroyed is negativity, an action that is necessary in order for great creation and transformation to occur. At all moments that require important transformation, Kali is there. She gives our life true meaning and purpose by offering depth and feeling.

It is considered that Kali is the cause of time as her name reflects this in that with *Kala* means "time" and *i*, "the cause". She was also considered to be beyond time. The following Tantrasara prayer addressed to Kali reinforces this belief:

"O Mother Cause and Mother of the World!
Thou art the One Primordial Being,
Mother of innumerable creatures,

> Creatrix of the very Gods;
> Even of Brahma the Creator, Vishnu the Preserver, and Shiva
>     the Destroyer!
> O Mother, in hymning thy praise I purify my speech."[80]

Kali commands the three *gunas*, threads of creation, preservation, and destruction that are not only a connection to the three gods mentioned in the above Tantrasara prayer, but embody the past, present, and future. These gunas are symbolised by white, red, and black threads, which in turn are each depicted in the images of Kali – her black skin, her red lolling tongue and her white teeth. Being the creatrix of existence, Kali's world is an eternal living flux from which all things rise and disappear over and over again in endless cycles. The gods whom she bore and devoured address Kali as:

> "Thou art the Original of all the manifestations;
> Thou art the birthplace of even Us;
> Thou knowest the whole world, yet none know Thee
> Thou art both Subtle and Gross, Manifested and Veiled,
> Formless, yet with form.
> Who can understand Thee?
> It is Thou who art the Supreme Primordial Kalika
> Resuming after dissolution Thine own form, dark and
>     formless.
> Thou alone remainest as One ineffable and inconceivable
> Though Thy self without beginning, multiform by the power
>     of Maya,
> Thou art the Beginning of all, Creatrix, Protectress, and
>     Destructress."[81]

Kali appears in various forms as an embodiment of Shakti, the eternal feminine energy and cosmic power. She is believed to be the eternal cosmic strength that destroys all existence. Her terrifying facial expressions depict the extent of her powers of destruction. The head she holds in her hand instantly arouses fear, and her protruding tongue symbolizes the mockery of human ignorance.

Within Hindu mythology, Kali came into being after Brahma, the god responsible for all creation, granted a boon to the demon Raktavij in that for every drop of his blood that fell on the ground, hundreds of demons like him would be produced. Therefore, the only way of slaying Raktavij was by not allowing any of his blood to touch the ground. One day the giants Sumbha and Nisumbha, equipped with powerful armies, marched against the demigods. In terror, the demigods approached Lord Shiva for help. However, as the giants were also his devotees, he was not able to assist. Instead Lord Shiva suggested that his consort, Parvati, be approached.

To aid the demigods, Parvati appeared as the ferocious warrior goddess Durga and quickly vanquished the giants' army. Sumbha and Nisumbha then marched with a second army led by Raktavij. Durga fiercely attacked the demon. However, from each drop of Raktavji's blood that touched the earth, a hundred more demons, just as strong, appeared. Nearing defeat, Durga desperately split herself in two and the part that became Kali drank the drops of blood before they touched the earth. Soon Raktavij was dead and the rest of the army, including Sumbha and Nisumbha, were defeated. Kali, however, had developed a taste for blood and a blind lust for destruction. In order to stop the world from being destroyed, Lord Shiva had to intervene.

Seeing no other way of dissuading her, Lord Shiva threw himself amongst the bodies of slain demons at the feet of Kali. Upon sensing her consort beneath her feet, Kali stopped her dance of destruction, and by returning to her guise as the passive Parvati, the world was saved.

According to other myths, Kali and Lord Shiva were the originating couple of the universe. However, Kali is also considered to be the unique source of everything. In this latter version, Kali is the full spectrum of universal power – both the benign and terrible mother. She nurtures and creates, yet she also destroys. As the Kalika (the Crone), Kali governs every form of death but also rules every form of life. She represents the three divisions of the Hindu year, the three phases of the moon, the three sections of the cosmos, and the three stages of life. There are even three types of priestesses who attend her shrines: *Yoginis* or *Shaktis* (the "Maidens"), *Matri* (the "Mothers"); and *Dakinis* (the "Skywalkers"). This latter group attends the dying, govern funerary rites and act as angels of death.[82]

For Kali devotees it is said that if one cannot love Kali's dark face, then one cannot hope to become enlightened. Tantric worshippers believe it is essential to face her curse, the terror of death, as willingly as they accept blessings from Kali's beautiful, nurturing, maternal aspect. For them, wisdom means learning that no coin has only one side: death cannot exist without life, likewise life cannot exist without death.

From the canons of orthodox Hinduism, Kali, Durga, Parvati, Lakshmi and Saraswati are all different forms of the ultimate power that are revered on different occasions. Kali represents the crude powers to fight evil, and the core strength required to battle enemies.

We are living in "Kali Yuga", the age of vice where the Dark Goddess is preparing to devour and destroy the world as people have moved as far away from "God" (spirituality) as possible.[83] To the Hindu devotee, performing a puja (a rite of reverence through invocations, prayers and songs) is a way of making a spiritual connection. When performing a Kali Puja[84] the goddess is called upon to help destroy "evil" - to diminish the ego and all negative tendencies that hinder spiritual progress and material prosperity.

Kali's revelation in and through the acceptance of her totality. The blade and head are offered to the goddess as a desire to be released from detachments as well as the limitations and constraints of our egos. To take only half of Kali is to miss the whole point entirely.

Kali is a powerful goddess to work with as she takes no prisoners, so to speak. She is more than happy to cut through illusion, but there is an air of caution when working with her that Kali-Ma (as she is often referred to by devotees) will bring about the "truth" which may not be what we actually perceive. This is the "universal" truth, our soul truth, that she brings, and we may find ourselves in places of pain and disassociation as familiar illusions are removed from our lives.

If anything, Kali teaches us to stand up and own our actions, to take a deep look at ourselves and the life direction we are heading in, and to stop playing the victim. We need to take responsibility from this point onwards as to how we live our life.

## Working with Kali

One way to evoke Kali in order to bring ourselves into balance or alignment with respect to a specific situation is through the use of her mantra. As the results can be dramatic and even unpleasant, it is strongly recommended that openness is undertaken for what will be received. For instance, if you are having problems with a relationship and use Kali's mantra to help with the problem, the relationship may end abruptly, even though this may not the outcome you desired. Whatever the issue, Kali gets right to the point and lets your ego attachments fall where they may.

The following mantra is believed to bring rapid and even drastic relief from situations that appear to be difficult or problematic. Utilising the word "krim", the seed of transformation that is exclusively associated with Kali Ma, should be used with care. This is because the solution attained through the use of this mantra may not be what you would want or envisage; instead the results will be right and appropriate for you at the time, although they may not be pleasant in the short term. The mantra means "Om and salutations. I attract she who is dark and powerful". It should be repeated until you feel the presence of the goddess, or at least 108 times[85].

*Om Klim Kalika-yei Namaha.*
(Pronounced: Om Kleem, Kaa-Lee-Kaa-Yay Naa-Maa-Haa)

It should be pointed out that, when called upon, Kali does cut things from your life without giving a second thought. Her actions can be extremely swift and come without warning or with no time for you to consider any possible complications. Therefore, there is not any time for second guessing or changing your mind. You need to be solid in your resolve and prepared to take ownership of the consequences as they may not always result in ways you may initially expect.

## Invocation to Kali

Om krim, I call to thee, O Divine Mother Kali, for your strength and destructive power.

Destroy the barriers of ignorance I have erected

And open the doors to your great mysteries.

Om krim, I call to thee, O Divine Mother Kali, for your fertility and compassion.

Inspire in me the creative potential and ability to face my challenges

And grow from them in new and positive ways.

Om krim, I call to thee, O Divine Mother Kali, for your gift of great sleep and rebirth.

Enable me to see beyond the veils of limited existence

And to understand the mysteries that reside beyond creation and destruction.

It is you, O Divine Mother Kali, who is the intrinsic nature of consciousness.

It is you, O Divine Mother Kali, who is the form of bliss

and blisslessness.

It is you, O Divine Mother Kali, who is the great elements of existence as they unite in forms and in their ununited individual aspects as well.

You who are in the waters of the inner ocean.

You who are above and below and even beyond.

You who are the entire perceivable universe.

Beloved Mother, I call to thee

Om Kali, Om Kali, Om Kali, Om.

## Correspondences associated with Kali

Snakes, bees, jackals, skulls, blood, cosmos, gold, black and sometimes white colours, red hibiscus flowers, frankincense, sandalwood, rose, red wine, menstrual blood, scimitar or sword, trident, head, bowl.

## Meditation: Cutting Through Illusion

You find yourself in a bustling marketplace, piles of spices and colourful sari wearing women indicate that you are in India. Pause and take in the sights, the sounds and the scents around you as people jostle past. East of you the sun is shining and growing in strength. In the distance, on the hillside, you can make out a walled structure and automatically feel yourself being drawn to it. Carefully stepping around the cars and sacred cows, you begin to make your way through the busy yet dusty streets, and somewhere in the distance you hear a bell ringing as if it is calling you.

The scents and sounds of the market place fade as you walk further and further away from it, while moving closer and closer towards the walled structure, following a dusty path. Eventually you come to the structure and realise it is a cemetery that is still being used to burn the bodies of those who have died. Run your fingers along the wall, feeling the rough stone structure beneath your fingertips. You come to an ornate wrought iron gate and as you step through into the cemetery grounds you notice a small enclosure in the stone wall where someone has placed a bunch of deep red roses.

Take in your surroundings once again. The scene inside the walled cemetery may shock you as there are many bodies being burnt, and amongst the smoke, the wails of the mourners can be heard. Ahead of you, through the smoke, you make out another structure, this time it is a stone tower at the far back corner of the cemetery that you feel drawn to. As you walk towards it, you do not linger, allowing the confronting sights, sounds and smells drift over and around you. Once inside the stone building, you realise it is a shrine to Kali-Ma, the Hindu goddess of death and destruction. Facing you is a simple altar holding an image of the goddess surrounded by red rose petals. To the right of the image is a vase containing red roses and to the left a golden chalice filled with red wine. In front of the image there is a bowl filled with red kumu, a sacred powder to mark the centre of your forehead.

You kneel before the altar, and with your dominant hand, dip your forefinger into the bowl of kumu and make a mark in the middle of your forehead with the powder. You take a rose from the vase and as you break open the flower, you gently scatter the petals in front of the image. Finally you take a sip from the chalice and as you replace it back onto the altar, you savour the fruity taste on your tongue.

From the shadows to the right of the altar you notice a woman emerging, dressed in a red sari that covers her dark coloured skin. Catching your eye, she smiles and you are surprised by the whiteness of her teeth. Instinctively you realise that she is Kali. In one of her many hands she holds her sacred scimitar, a double-edged sword. You know that she has the power to slay demons, yet she also has the ability to be extremely compassionate. You realise that sometimes demons are our illusion and fantasies about life. Sometimes we do not see things for what they really are, or we disguise our own destructive anger from our own selves. You acknowledge that during such times it is necessary to allow Kali to take her sword and cut through the illusions that protect us from seeing and acting on the truth.

The Hindu Dark Goddess begins to sway and move around you, swinging her mighty sword, cutting through all the illusions that have been created around you, slicing back to the hard-core truth and exposing your authentic self. As she moves around you, the aroma of rose and sandalwood fills the air. Kali begins to slice through negative thoughts and old outdated emotional attachments that have been holding you back, and as this happens, you feel a release as these begin to fall away from you. You close your eyes and focus on the scent, breathing in deeply and surrendering to the process. You feel the negativity release itself from you and its hold upon your life. You embrace the moment when Kali approaches you and slices away the unwanted, releasing you from the hindrances of the past. As this occurs, you are anointed with an oil that is sacred to Kali made from rose and sandalwood and you focus on the scent and embrace the release.

After a while you realise you can no longer smell the rose and sandalwood. As you open your eyes, you find yourself alone before the altar in the stone shrine. Kali is nowhere in sight. You remain seated, gathering your thoughts and notice that you feel lighter than you did when you entered the shrine. Your gaze falls onto the image of Kali on the altar and you instinctively bring your hands together in a prayer position, bowing your head with thanks and gratitude for what you have undergone.

Slowly you rise to your feet again and leave the stone shrine, carefully making your way back through the cemetery to the wrought iron gates. You notice the sun is now in the western portion of the sky and that its power has decreased. Once again you notice a small enclosure in the stone wall by the gate and this time in place of the red roses there is a scroll. Instinctively you know that this is a message from Kali for you. As you unroll the scroll, take note of what is written on it as it will be a personal message just for you.

When you are ready, follow the dusty path back to your starting place. With each step you take you become more and more aware of the physical world around you, your physical body and your breathing as you inhale and exhale. With each breath, continue to bring your awareness to the here and now, and when you are ready, open your eyes.

# Oya: Mother of the Nine

*Oya who causes the leaves to flutter*
*Oya, strong wind who gave birth to fire while traversing the*
*mountain*
*Oya, please don't fell the tree in my backyard*
*Oya, we have seen fire covering your body like cloth.*[86]

In Africa, Oya is a Yoruban *orisha* (divine being, likened to that of a god or goddess) of weather (in particular tornadoes and lightning), fire, destructive rainstorms, female leadership, persuasive charm and transformation. She is the "Queen of the Marketplace", a shrewd businesswoman, as well as being the primordial Mother of Chaos. She is the "Wild Wind" as she is the first breath as well as the last which carries the spirits of the dead to the Other World, and the "Keeper of the Cemetery" with the graveyard her home and the spirits of the dead her subjects.

Oya was said to have wedded Ogun while in the form of a buffalo, and that she stole his weapons of war, replacing them with farm implements. One day she dipped her finger into a medicine gourd belonging to Ogun's younger and more handsome brother, Shango, the God of Thunder, and started to shoot fire and lightening from her mouth whenever she spoke. From that day onwards, she used her forked lightening to help Shango fight his battles. After running away with Shango, Ogun was said to have broken Oya into nine pieces and became known as the "Mother of Nine". Other myths indicate she was given this title for being the guardian of the Niger River (which has nine tributaries), or alternatively, as the keeper of a "Sacred Cloth of many Colours" (that was said to hold the wisdom of all women), there were nine daughters that Oya bestowed this cloth upon.

In her partnership with Shango, Oya complemented him despite actually being his third wife (the first two being Oba and Oshun). As the God of Thunder, Shango would hurl thunderstones to earth killing anyone who offended him, or he would set their house on fire. When Shango wanted to fight with lightning, he would send Oya ahead of him where she would manifest as a strong wind preceding a thunderstorm blowing the rooves off houses and knocking down large trees. Oya would also fan any fires set by the thunderbolts that Shango had thrown. When the strong winds of Oya came, the Yoruban people knew that Shango was not far behind, and it is said that without her, Shango would not be able to fight. This made Oya to be considered actually fiercer than her husband.[87] The two never lived together, as Oya preferred her forest and Shango was possibly already traumatized from the rivalry between Oba and Oshun that caused him to banish both of them.

Another myth records that Oya was originally an antelope who would transform herself into a beautiful woman every five days by removing her antelope skin and hiding it under a scrub near a marketplace. One day Shango met this beautiful woman in the market and being so struck by her beauty, he followed her into the forest where he watched as she donned the skin, turning herself back into an antelope.

The next day Shango hid himself in the forest, and when Oya removed the skin and had gone into the market, he picked it up and took it home where he hid it in the rafters. However, Shango's other wives became jealous of Oya after she bore Shango twins, that they told her where the skin was hanging. Oya then donned the skin, returning once more to her antelope form, before disappearing into the forest.[88]

As the "Mother of the Elders of the Night", Oya was perceived to be a sorceress of the magical arts who aided in all forms of divination and intuition. Dark as night, she was found dwelling in the cemeteries where the ancestors awaited to assist family and loved ones who crossed over.

In Yoruban tradition, Oya was both loved and feared as her

mysteries were passed from daughter to daughter. As well as preserving the healing arts, her worship was associated with celebrating the ancient mothers to ensure the continuation of power through the family lines. Through dance and ritual, the women would celebrate Oya, calling forth vision and power of the self through blood and the vulva, with the latter representing their connection to the goddess. They would call to Oya who would appear whirling a beaded horsetail and sabre, a tool to cut away injustice and deceit; the horsetail symbolising power and integrity of a wise woman.

Fiercely protective as a mother and an aspect of the Dark Goddess, Oya is not a goddess to call upon lightly. She is a fierce warrior and protectress of woman who call to her in order to settle disputes in their favour. Oya demands the devotee to be strong, honorable and true to her own self. Wielding her machete, or sword of truth, to cut through stagnation, Oya will clear the way for new growth. She can be likened to the Hindu goddess Kali.

As the only Orisha who has power over the dead, cemeteries are known as *ile yansan*, or "Oya's house". She also shows a compassionate side by allowing dying children to live as a gift to their parents. Anyone who uses dead bodies or parts of dead bodies in their ceremonies must render payment and homage to Oya, and whenever there is a haunting Oya is summoned to dismiss the spirit.

It is said that Oya has such a terrible face that anyone looking at her will be stricken mad or go blind. In ceremonies where Oya descends no one should look upon her. When she possesses someone she puts on a red crepe dress or a flowered dress and weaves multi-coloured ribbon around her head. When her "children" (or devotees) enter trance states, some of them are even able to handle live coals with their bare hands.

## Working with Oya

Oya is often depicted being dressed in her favourite colours of purple, dark burgundy or maroon, yet she is also symbolized by nine colours: purple, blue, green yellow, orange, red, black, white and brown. While she may embrace the practitioner in her storms of change she will also strike you down with her lightning should the need arise, for she is also a goddess of fertility capable of stripping away what must die in order for the harvest to be abundant.

The following is a prayer entitled "Oriki Oya"[89] (praising the spirit of the wind) that forms part of the American based Iwa Pele Training School providing guidance with respect to style of divination referred to as "ifa" within the Yoruba culture that consists of a number of prayer cycles:

*Oya aroju ba oko gu o palemo bara – bara.*

*Afefe iku. Abesan wo ebiti kosunwon efufu lele ti nbe igi ilekun ile anan.*

(Spirit of the Wind died courageously with her husband, she puts matters in order suddenly.

The wind of death. Mother of nine shatters the evil mound of earth, strong wind demolishes the tree by the family door.)

*Okiki a gbo oke so edun, igan obinrin ti nko ida,*

*Oya iji ti se tit bajo – bajo.*

(Rumour in the clouds, hurls down a stone axe, courageous woman armed forever with a sword, Spirit of the Wind, tornado, sets the leaves of the trees in motion.)

*A pa kete, bo kete.*

*Ase.*

(She kills suddenly, she enters suddenly.

May it be so.)

## Invocation to Oya

I call to thee, O mighty Oya
She who is the Lady of Storms
She who is the Bringer of Change
She who is the Warrior of all Women.
Oya is your name.
Oya! Your name calls the winds.
Oya! Your name weighs the truth.
Oya! Your name comforts the dead.
I call to thee, O mighty Oya.
Bring to me the positive change needed in my life.
Bring to me the action I seek to make these changes
Bring to me your strength and grace to accept these changes
I call to thee, O mighty Oya.
Lady of Storms, Bringer of Change
She who is most powerful.
Bring to me your wisdom of change.

## Correspondences associated with Oya

Aubergines (eggplants), beets, sesame seeds, chick peas, red wine, purple grapes, deep burgundy and purple colours, lightning bolts, graves, masks, benzoin resin, lavender, mugwort, peppermint, wormwood, water buffalo, garnet, amethyst, black opal.

## Meditation: Winds of Change

Imagine you are standing on the foreshore looking out across the ocean where there is a storm brewing. In your hands you hold nine coins. Before you are a number of images drawn in the sand, each of which representing some aspect of yourself that is in need of change, whether it be attitudes and perceptions, how you view yourself, your diet, relationships with the various people in your life past and present, what you do to financially support yourself, your work/life balance, and the like.

As the clouds grow larger and darker, they roll across the sky towards you. You feel the gentle breeze increase in strength. The clouds that were once white and fluffy drifting across the blue sky, are now dark grey, bordering black, hanging heavy and looking threatening as they approach closer and closer. The wind continues to increase and you feel it tugging at your hair.

In the centre, or eye, of the approaching darkness there is a large deep burgundy and purple swirling mass. This is Oya, the Yoruban Orisha of the winds and of personal change. These are her winds of change rolling in toward you. The swirling colours appear to be her skirts, or are you imagining things? The wind continues to grow and you feel it tugging now at your clothes. You lean into it in an effort to keep standing on your feet. It is a struggle, but somehow you manage to stand on your own feet. And all the while, you push aside the need to flee and seek cover. Something is making you stand and embrace the change that is coming your way.

The swirling deep burgundy and purple mass is almost upon you and from its centre, the eye of the storm, you notice that a shape has formed, that of a beautiful woman with dark brown skin and even darker eyes. She speaks not a word to you, only motions you to look down at the images drawn in the sand before you. You notice that not all of the images remain, some may have even changed. Others have completely blown away.

Your eyes meet Oya's and she smiles knowingly, for it is her winds that have activated the much needed change in your life. Lightning cracks along the foreshore as if it is providing you with the needed power and energy to follow through with these changes.

You offer the coins to Oya and as you do, the winds tug at your hair again. Suddenly the orisha is gone and with her the coins. As the wind subsides you notice a rainbow forming over the water. It is a sign of blessing from Oya that your offering has been accepted.

# Hekate of the Crossroads

*I call Ækáti of the Crossroads, worshipped at the meeting of three*
*paths, oh lovely one.*
*In the sky, earth, and sea, you are venerated in your*
*saffron-colored robes.*
*Funereal Daimohn, celebrating among the souls of those who*
*have passed.*
*Persian, fond of deserted places, you delight in deer.*
*Goddess of night, protectress of dogs, invincible Queen.*[90]

Contrary to popular belief, Hekate was not originally a Greek goddess, nor was she an aged crone. This connection appears to have stemmed back to Jane Harrison's *Prolegomena to the Study of Greek Religion* and later Robert Graves' poetic work *The White Goddess* (as indicated in the introduction) and with Hekate's connection with the Underworld being associated with the dark phase of the moon and therefore the crone goddess.

Hekate's roots seem to originate in the city of Lagina in Carian (modern day Turkey) where a ceremony *kleidos agoge* ("procession of the key") was held at her major temple making her a tutelary goddess[91]. Hekate was then later naturalised in Mycenaean Greece in the province of Thrace.

Greek poet Hesiod is one of our best sources for information about Hekate. In *Theogony* (a book about the lineage of the Olympian gods), he claimed that Hekate was the daughter of the Titan Perses and Asteria (a star goddess who was the sister of Leto, the mother of Artemis and Apollo). The grandmother of these three cousins was Phoebe, the ancient Titaness who personified the moon. According to Hesiod, Hekate was a reappearance of Phoebe, the moon goddess herself, who appeared during the dark of the moon. Hesiod also made a detailed description of Hekate's significance to the Olympian gods:

"... Hekate, whom Zeus honoured above all others; he gave her dazzling gifts, a share of the earth and a share of the barren sea. She was given a place of honour in the starry sky, and among the deathless gods her rank is high. For even now, when a mortal propitiates the Gods and, following custom, sacrifices well-chosen victims, he invokes Hekate, and if she receives his prayers with favour, then honour goes to him with great ease, and he is given blessings, because she has power and a share in all the rights once granted to the offspring of Ouranos and Gaia."[92]

From ancient Greek myth two versions of Hekate have emerged. In a lesser role, Hekate was a mortal priestess associated with Iphigeneia, who scorned and insulted Artemis, eventually leading to her suicide. Artemis then adorned the dead body with jewellery and whispered for her spirit to rise to become her "Hekate", which acted as an avenging spirit for injured women. Such myths where a deity sponsors or "creates" a foreign one were widespread in ancient cultures as a way of integrating foreign cults. Additionally, as Hekate's cult grew, her figure was added to the later myth of the birth of Zeus as one of the midwives who hid the child, while Cronus consumed the deceiving rock handed to him by Gaia.

The second version explained how Hekate gains the title of the "Queen of Ghosts" and her role as a goddess of sorcery. Like totems of Hermes that were placed at borders as a ward against danger, images of Hekate would also serve in such a protective role. It became common to place statues of the goddess at the gates of cities, and eventually domestic doorways. Over time, the association of keeping out evil spirits led to the belief that, if offended, Hekate could also let in evil spirits. Thus, invocations to Hekate arose as the supreme governess of the borders between the normal world and the spirit world.

By the 5th century CE Hekate was perceived as a Great

Goddess as well as a mistress of witchcraft and sorcery. Medea, a priestess of Hekate, was able to assist the hero Jason through her knowledge of the paths of the stars and the moon in the night sky, as well as her skill using magic herbs and potions. Circe, sometimes described as Hekate's daughter by the sun god Helios, was said to have turned Odysseus' crew into animals by her knowledge of sorcery and herb magic.

Although she was never truly incorporated among the Olympian deities, the modern understanding of Hekate may have been derived from the Hellenistic culture of Alexandria in Egypt. In the magical papyri of Ptolemaic Egypt, she is called the "she-dog" or bitch, with the barking of dogs signifying her presence. She sustained a large following as a goddess of protection and childbirth. In later imagery, Hekate had two ghostly dogs, or even a pack of red eyed hell hounds as servants by her side. This has led to the belief that Hekate was visible only to dogs, and if dogs howl in the night, it meant that she was about.

Hekate has been associated with many incantations, sacrifices and rituals throughout history. In ancient times, people sought to appease her by leaving chicken hearts and honey cakes outside their doors. On the last day of the month offerings of honey, onions, fish and eggs were left at crossroads, along with sacrifices of puppies, infant girls and female-lambs. Sorcerers gathered at crossroads to pay homage to her and such infernal servants as the *Empusa* (a hobgoblin), the *Cercopsis* (a poltergeist), and the *Mormo* (ghoul). The following is a petition of her patronae recorded in the 3rd century by Hippolytus of Rome, one of the most important theologians at the time:

"Come infernal, terrestrial, and heavenly Bombo [Hekate],
Goddess of the broad roadways, of the crossroad,
thou who goest to and fro at night, torch in hand, enemy of
the day.

Friend and lover of darkness,
thou who doest rejoice when the bitches are howling
and warm blood is spilled,
thou who art walking amid the phantoms and in the place of
tombs,
thou whose thirst is blood, thou who doest strike chill fear
into mortal hearts.
Gorgo, Mormo, Moon of a thousand forms,
cast a propitious eye upon our sacrifice."[93]

Over the millennium numerous epithets have been given to Hekate, some of the more commonly known ones are listed below. The first three of these epithets are Hekate's most distinctive functions, and generally involve her attending upon other deities including Demeter, Persephone, Artemis, and Cybele. The last two titles, on the other hand, are shared with numerous other deities found within the Greek pantheon. It does not seem possible to rank these functions as to their importance; different ones were emphasized at different times and locations.

- Hekate *Propylaia,* "the one before the gate": A guardian goddess whose statue was often at the entrance to major temples of other deities, primarily Demeter, or at the entrance to private homes.
- Hekate *Propolos,* "the attendant who leads": A personal attendant and guide, the most famous example of which is when she leads Persephone back to Demeter from the Underworld.
- Hekate *Phosphoros,* "the light bringer": A torchbearer (probably related to her role as guide, especially one who guides and attends initiates at the mysteries, such as the Eleusinian Mysteries). While other deities carried a single torch, Hekate was most prominently associated with carrying two.

- Hekate *Kourotrophos*, "child's nurse": A title applied to nearly all goddesses who govern childbirth. It may refer to a maternal caring for all mortal beings and may possibly refer to caring for women specifically.
- Hekate *Chthonia*, "of the earth": The word "chthonia" in mythology points to earth as Source, as Mother of all living, or to our earliest understandings of creation and creator.

The *Greek Magical Papyri*, produced between the 2nd century BCE and 5th century CE, contained a collection of ancient rituals, prayers and spells from Graeco-Roman Egypt that mentioned Hekate in her various Underworld aspects including *Drakaina* (of dragons), *Kardiodaitos* (eater of men's hearts), and *Nekyia* (Mistress of Corpses).

Other epithets of Hekate include *Crataeis* (the Mighty One), *Kleidouchos* (you who hold all keys and grant all answers), *Trikephalus* "triple headed goddess), *Soteira* (protect), *Prytania* (Unconquerable Goddess of the Mighty Dead), *Trimorphos* (Goddess of Earth, Heaven and the Underworld), *Nocticula* (let your thousand shifting forms reveal their mysteries), *Enodia* (Goddess of all Hidden Pathways), and *Trioditis* (Goddess of the Crossroads).

## Working with Hekate

The triple faced Hekate stands at the crossroads of our unconscious and this makes her an aspect of the Dark Goddess. When honoured, she bestows gifts of inspiration, vision, magic and regeneration. It is she who holds the key that unlocks the doors to the subconscious. She bears the torch that illuminates both the treasures and terrors of the unconscious. She guides us through the dark spirit world wherein we can receive a revelation of meaning. She also shows us that the way out is to ride on the surge of renewal.

## Invocation to Hekate

Come to me, O beloved mistress
Three-faced Hekate of the midnight skies
Dawn-born light-bringer who rides to fierce eyed bulls
Come to me, Hekate, I call to thee.
You who are the moon engulfed by the obsidian veil
The beauty of the stars on high.
It is you who I hear in the silence of night
Comforting the darkness within my soul.
Come to me, O beloved keeper of the keys
Goddess of the phantoms and ill-lit spaces
It is from you that all Gods and men were born
The holder of the sacred mysteries that I seek.
Come to me, Hekate, I call to thee.
Hear my plea and bless me with your presence.

## Correspondences associated with Hekate

Snakes, owls, hounds, torches, keys, crossroads, the dark or new moon, red and black colours, poppy seeds, black onyx, black obsidian, belladonna, garlic, sandalwood, cypress, myrrh.

## Meditation: Meeting Hekate of the Crossroads

Pass through the mists and darkness and find yourself standing at the crossroad at night, with three paths splitting in three different directions before you. Study the paths to see which one to choose. Behind you someone is moving, pacing up and down. You turn and notice a dark veiled figure. This is Hekate. She is the guide of the souls through deep unfathomable places of the psyche. She stands quietly at the threshold unseen until she hears the soul-cry of those who ask her to light the way. She now stands silently before you, carrying a mirror.

She then speaks: "I wait in the darkness of the moonless night with my hounds at the crossroads, a place where three roads converge, a place of choice. All paths that lead to the crossroads are desirable, but only one can you travel. Only one can you choose. Choice creates endings and all beginnings come from endings. Which road will you choose? Which way will you go? Although the choice is yours, here is a secret that I will share: The way to choose is to enter the void. The way to choose is to let die. The way to choose is to fly free."

She holds up her mirror for you to look in to. What do you see? If you see nothing in the mirror, Hekate will whisper something in your ear. Whatever you see or hear, it will be the answer you need for now.

# Persephone: Queen of the Shadows

*Persephone, Daughter of Zeus, blessed*
*Only begotten, gracious goddess, receive this good offering,*
*Much honoured, you, overpowered by Pluto, you are beloved and*
*lifegiving,*
*You hold the doors of Hades under the depths of the earth;*
*Transactor of Justice, your beloved hair the sacred olive branch of the*
*enemy*
*Mother of the Eumenides, Queen of the Underworld,*
*You, maiden from Zeus through secret begetting.*[94]

The myth of the abduction of Persephone is one of the oldest of all Greek myths. Her story is a personification of some of the most universal concepts about life and death. In her youth, Persephone represents the powerful bond between a mother and a daughter and the often-difficult transition from maidenhood to marriage. As the goddess of springtime and rebirth, she is eternally connected to the cycles of the earth, which lies barren in her absence and blooms again each spring with her return. Her initiatory experience in the realm of the dead is such a powerful experience that it changes her life forever. It is after this transformation that we remember her most for her role as the Greek goddess and Queen of the Underworld.

According to myth, Persephone was the only daughter of Demeter, the grain goddess, and was also known as *Kore* (meaning "maiden"). She was abducted by Hades (in some accounts also raped) and taken into the Underworld when she was out picking flowers one day with some friends when a narcissus caught her eye. As she reached to pick it, the ground opened up and Hades, the God of the Underworld, rode forth on his chariot, and snatched the maiden before he returned to his abode. When she discovered her daughter was missing, Demeter went into mourning, neglecting her obligations and the people of earth were not able to harvest their crops and started to starve. This also mean they were not able to make any offerings to the gods. It was only then that Zeus stepped in and confronted his brother.

When Hades refused to give up his new bride in order for the gods to be able to receive their offerings, a bargain was struck that the daughter of Demeter was allowed to be released providing that she had not eaten anything from the Underworld. However, she had eaten three seeds from the pomegranate and so the maiden Kore became Persephone, the Queen of the Underworld. It was these three tiny pomegranate seeds that bound her forever to the Underworld, her own realm.

American author on social criticism, Charlene Spretnak[95], points to the fact that this myth appeared prior to the invasion of Greece that resulted in establishing the Olympian gods and the original myth records that Persephone volunteered to go into the Underworld in order to help the lost souls. This interpretation makes the myth her coming of age, where she was stepping away from the bonds of her mother and establishing her own place in the world. After all, why would such a powerful goddess as Persephone allow herself to be kidnapped in the first place?

Other authors interpreting the myth tend to retain the more familiar version (as outlined above) and focus on the symbolism contained within, in particular the eating of the pomegranate seeds that forced (or enabled) Persephone to remain in the Underworld where she shed the labels and attachments, as well as any expectations of others, that had been placed upon her. In doing so, this action moved her away from being referred to as simply Kore, the daughter of Demeter, to Persephone, a queen in her own right and her transition between childhood and womanhood, where she was able to make her own decisions and therefore able to stand on her own two feet. This transition from Kore to Persephone can also been seen as two very different personifications of the same deity, where the springtime goddess (Kore) also takes on the role of the winter goddess of the Underworld (Persephone). Some historians see this double role in black and white terms: "One of her forms (daughter with mother) appears as life; the other (young girl with husband) as death"[96]. The ability to integrate all these aspects of her dualistic life as wife and daughter, innocence and wisdom, death and rebirth are what makes Persephone such a powerful goddess.

Other interpretations of her story focus on Persephone as one aspect of the triple goddess, a powerful feminine archetype where Maiden, Mother and Crone are seen as one. While the three parts of this trinity are sometimes seen as Kore, Demeter and Persephone, many modern authors focus on Demeter and Persephone's relationship with the dark moon goddess, Hekate. In the *Hymn to Demeter*, Hekate is the only one, besides the sun god, Helios, to hear Kore's cries during her abduction. When Persephone returns from the Underworld, Hekate vows to serve her as her "chief attendant". Feminist author Patricia Monaghan explains that "the Greek world was divided into three parts, in honour of the threefold goddess, with Hekate wandering the sky, Demeter ruling the surface of the earth, and Persephone ruling the world of the afterlife."[97]

During Persephone's absence, Demeter lost all interest in her duties as the goddess of grain and agriculture. She roamed the earth in search of her daughter for nine days (or months). In the *Hymn to Demeter*, it is not until after she has travelled to Eleusis that Persephone's mother is finally overcome with such rage and depression that "for mortals she ordained a terrible and brutal year on the deeply fertile earth. The ground released no seed, for bright-crowned Demeter kept it buried."[98] In any case, the barren landscape is what sets the stage for Persephone to return again each spring as the goddess of rebirth.

Persephone's reunion with her mother is bittersweet. She has consumed the fruit of the dead, the pomegranate, either of her own accord or as a trick by Hades. In any case, she has been transformed and will be forced to stay at least part of each year in his domain. Most stories say she stays there for three months every winter, at which time Demeter mourns and lets the earth go bare. Other stories tell of a six-month absence in the Underworld. Either way, life for the young goddess will never be the same. Persephone is now a wife and queen, who has been initiated into the mysteries of the Underworld. Interestingly, Persephone only eats these seeds just prior to her "release" from Hades' realm.

Spretnak, in her research of pre-Hellenic goddess myths, indicates that in the original story there was actually no mention of the goddess's abduction into the Underworld, and that Persephone is actually a psychopomp (conductor of souls into the Underworld).[99] While Greek philosophers such as Sophocles and Plato have acknowledged Persephone as a "welcomer of the dead", most myths do not tell this aspect in her story. Spretnak's version of the myth also has Persephone explaining to her mother that there are spirits who "drift about restlessly" and "hover around their earthly homes" because they do not understand their state. She then volunteers to go down to the Underworld and initiate them into their new life. While at first resisting Persephone's desire, Demeter comes to understand her motives and leads her to "a long, deep chasm and produces a torch for her to carry".[100] When Persephone finally arrives in the Underworld, she stands on a rock, with her torch, a vase of her mother's grain, and a large bowl of "pomegranate seeds, the food of the dead". As her aura increases in "brightness and warmth", she introduces herself as Queen of the Dead, and explains to the spirits that they have left their earthly bodies. She then beckons "those nearest to step up onto the rock and enter her aura", where she embraces them, looks into their eyes, feeds them pomegranate seeds, and offers them a blessing for renewed "tranquillity and wisdom".[101]

For the modern reader, it is Persephone's time in the Underworld that interests us most. Here she is Hades' queen, ruling as his equal. As the Queen of the Underworld, Persephone is often portrayed as a force to be feared. In Homer's *Iliad* (written c.750-725 BCE) she is described as "grim Persephone" in direct contrast to Hades who is described as the "mighty Zeus of the Underworld". In Homer's other classic, *Odyssey* (written c.743-713 BCE), she has become "dread Persephone" or the "awesome one", whom mortal men mistrust. When Odysseus paid a visit to the House of Death, he worried that the vision of his dead mother, which slips through his fingers and "dissolves like a dream", is just "some wraith that great Persephone sends my way to make me ache with sorrow all the more?" But his noble mother answers: "This is no deception sent by Queen Persephone, this is just the way of mortals when we die". The goddess receives similar treatment in Hesiod's *Theogony* (c.700 BCE) where she is described as "awful Persephone", who is always at the side of "strong Hades". Neither of these classic works mentions anything about the life she led before becoming the Queen of the Dead or the radiant youthful beauty that attracts Hades enough to want her for his bride.

Persephone was viewed in more flattering light in later writings. The Homeric *Hymn to Demeter* (c.650-550 BCE) describes her as radiant, noble, and thoughtful. The Greek lyric poet Bacchylides (c.520-450 BCE) referred to the goddess as having "slender-ankles", and the tragic playwright Euripedes (c.480-406 BCE) sees her as "Persephone, fair young goddess of the netherworld". In addition, he brings up the duality of her nature and her relationship with her mother when he refers to her as "the goddess of twofold name, Persephone and the kindly goddess Demeter".

## Working with Persephone

Persephone reminds us of the importance to be adaptable in

whatever situation we find ourselves in for we never know where that situation may take us. She also reminds us to make the most of all that is presented to us – the good, the bad and even the most challenging situations. She appears to be the instigator of what happens to her. She was the one who picked the narcissus flower. She was also the one who ate the seeds from the pomegranate. Her lesson is also that without weakness and one cannot truly know strength and courage.[102]

## Invocation to Persephone

Hail to thee, Persephone, Queen of the Underworld
Daughter of Demeter and bride of Hades
It is you who guides the souls of the departed to their final
    rest.

Hail to thee, Persephone, the compassionate one
The keeper of dreams and reality we hide from
Yet in your arms we find comfort for our grief.

Hail to thee, Persephone, the Returning One
It is you who brings the prospect of spring
Encouraging us let go of the past, old dreams and fears.

Hail to thee, Persephone, maiden born now queen
Hail to thee, Persephone, hail.

## Correspondences associated with Persephone

Flower crown, torch, pomegranate, narcissus, hyacinth, willow tree, lily of the valley, lavender, wreath of flowers, mirror, red, indigo and black colours, peridot, green tourmaline, clear quartz, agate, black onyx, obsidian, agate.

## Meditation: Meeting the Queen of the Shadows

You are standing before the mouth of a cave when a woman

dressed in green robes approaches you, asking if you have seen her daughter. This is Demeter, the goddess of the earth, and she tells you how her only child was snatched by Hades, the lord of the Underworld. She begs for you to go into the Underworld and find out if her daughter will ever return to the upper world. You take pity upon Demeter and agree to do what she asks. Into your hand, Demeter places two silver coins and instructs that you are to give one of these coins to the ferryman for him to take you across the River Styx, and one to return.

You enter the cave and begin your journey downward, guided by a phosphorescent glow from the fungi growing on the walls. You hear rushing water and as the tunnel opens to a cavern, you notice you have come to the banks of a river where Charon, the ferryman, is waiting. Placing one coin into his hand as instructed, the ferryman pushes off from the bank and you glide effortlessly across the river to the other side.

Ahead is another tunnel that you enter and at the exit on the other side is the entrance to a large hall where two figures, one male and the other female, clad in black robes are sitting on thrones. As you approach, you notice the woman is extremely beautiful and appears to be a younger version of Demeter. This is Persephone, her daughter. Next to her sits the handsome yet sombre figure of Hades who regards you with deep penetrating eyes. They have been waiting for you and motion for you to approach.

You speak candidly to Persephone and Hades, advising them of your meeting with Demeter and why you are here, seeking information as to whether Persephone will return to the upper world. Persephone sighs and then smiles, gazing briefly at Hades before she speaks. Yes, while she was initially taken by force, she is happy being the Queen of the Underworld where she is ruler in her own right. As she speaks you notice she has placed her hand on his as a sign of affection.

Hades offers her the pomegranate which she eats willingly

and with full knowledge that it will bind her to his Underworld realm. Persephone asks you to return with a message for her mother Demeter that while she will return to bring spring to the upper world, it is here that she will spend most of her time now, as its queen.

When Persephone has finished talking, Hades points to a circular mirror on the wall and asks you if you would like to scry in it. This is a special mirror that can show scenes from past, present and future, in either real or symbolic form. You stand before the mirror and see what it has to show you.

When you have finished scrying, Persephone and Hades bid you farewell, and you walk back to Charon on his boat. You hand him the second coin and are returned to the other side of the river where you make you way back up the tunnel to the mouth of the cave. Here Demeter is waiting for you.

You tell her what Persephone told you and while there are tears in her eyes, there is also an element of acceptance as Demeter thanks you for what you have done for her. As she disappears, you are alone at the entrance to the cave again. Take a couple of deep breaths and return to the here and now.

# Nephthys: The Egyptian Goddess of Silence

*O Nebt-Het, Giver of Life, breathe upon us Your radiance and love.*
*O You who were wedded, even as we, to the Dark side and yet were*
*able to break free,*
*help me to do the same.*
*Stand You behind me, even as You do for my Mother Auset and*
*breathe*
*Your freedom of thought upon me. Radiate my life to be free and*
*guide me into the*
*Light of my Father's ways, those of Ausar.*
("An Ammonite Prayer to Nebt-Het") [103]

The seemingly silent Nephthys (Nebt-Het to the ancient Egyptians) is often described as the "dark" sister to Isis's "light". Yet there is a common bond between them that can never be shaken, as Christine Downing reminds us in her book about sibling relationships, and that bond is the one of sisterhood, where our same-sex sibling is "the other most like ourselves of any creature in the world".[104] Downing also forms the opinion that same-sex siblings tend to reflect the two sides of one's personality, the ideal self and what psycho-analyst Carl Jung calls "shadow". Was this the case with Nephthys and her better-known sister?

Of all the "genealogies" recorded in ancient Egypt, it was the Ennead, the nine gods and goddesses from Heliopolis, that we are more familiar with today and in particular the version interpreted by Greek biographer Plutarch (46 – 120 CE) in his *De Iside et Osiride*. The Ennead comprised of the Sun God, Ra-Atum, who created Shu (the God of Air) and Tefnet (the goddess of moisture). From this pair came Geb (the earth god) and Nut (the sky goddess). Finally, out of their union, two sets of twins were formed - Osiris and Isis (who fell in love with each other while they were in Nut's womb), and Set and Nephthys (a pairing of convenience according to Plutarch. From the moment of her birth Nephthys was recorded as being born "in a shroud of mystery", with a caul cast over her face.[105]

Prior to Plutarch's interpretation, details about the two sets of twins and their significance were recorded in the *Pyramid Texts* (dating from 2,400 BCE, the Old Kingdom) and the *Coffin Texts* (dating from 2,000 BCE, the Middle Kingdom). Both of these sources differ somewhat from Plutarch's Hellenistic influenced account, particularly in the pairing of Nephthys with Set, whereby they appeared to have originally complemented each other. In the *Pyramid Text* the sets of twins related important geological features in the ancient Egyptian landscape at a time when the country was divided into Upper (southern) Egypt which was represented by Nephthys and Set, and Lower (northern) Egypt, represented by Isis and Osiris. Such an association led Professor Jessica Levai (of Bridgewater State University, USA) to suggest that the pairing occurred from 18th Dynasty of the New Kingdom (1,550-1,295 BCE) when Set fell out of favour.[106] Levai also reflected on the geological connection by referring to Osiris as the god of the Nile River and ruler of Egypt whereas Set was the god of the desert, the polar opposite. Osiris was married to Isis, goddess of the fertile earth that bound the river; whereas Nephthys related to that strip of land that served as border between the fertile valley and the sterile desert.[107] This contrasted Plutarch's interpretation as he focused on the paring of Nephthys and Set as being the "darker", or maleficent, couple compared to the "light", or beneficent couple that was Isis and Osiris.

Levai also formed the opinion that Nephthys may have originally been partnered with Set's benevolent aspect who was the killer of Apep (Apophis to the Greeks). This aspect of Set was believed to have been worshipped in the western oasis during the time of the Roman occupation (between 30 BCE and 4 CE), where he co-ruled with Nephthys.[108]

Despite having joined Nephthys with Set, Plutarch[109] indicated that her true love for her older brother Osiris was so great that she seduced him and from that union mothered the jackal headed God, Anubis. Such a comment has given rise to the interpretation that Nephthys was jealous of her sister's relationship as her own was unfulfilling. Fearing the wrath of Set, Nephthys abandoned her son, only to have him discovered and raised by Isis. A differing of opinion has arisen amongst scholars as to whether Nephthys seduced Osiris, or whether, due to his intoxicated state at the time, he was not able to notice the subtle differences between the two sisters. Some interpretations even state that Isis was fully aware of this liaison, so much so she gave them her blessing.

Philosopher, academic Edward Butler has challenged Plutarch's translation of the Osirian myth by pointing out that few indigenous Egyptian sources record Anubis as being fathered by Osiris. Instead, reference tends to favour the sun god Re (Ra). Contrary to this, however, is the title of "Onnophret" that was sometimes applied to Nephthys that was the feminine form of the Osirian epithet "Onnophris" (wn.nfr) meaning "the beautiful existent". This title appeared to indicate a possibly that at some stage Nephthys may have actually been Osiris's wife.[110] This discovery further raises the question as to whether Osiris actually joined with both sisters at some stage during the evolution of the myth.

Returning to the Osirian myth of Plutarch, the basis of this myth had already been established by the 24th century BCE (Egypt's Fifth Dynasty) where it focused around the death and resurrection of Osiris. Wanting to overtake his older brother's rule, Set (the God of Chaos and Destruction) tricked Osiris into climbing into a coffin, which was then thrown into the Nile River. Once this was located by Isis, Set subsequently dismembered Osiris's body, scattering the pieces across the country. Instead of taking her consort's side to play a part in the murderous plot and risking the wrath of his anger and jealousy, Nephthys aligned her loyalty with her sister, joining in the search for Osiris's scattered body parts. She also assisted in the revival and subsequent resurrection of the dead god. She later appeared in the mourning of Osiris alongside Isis.

As interesting as all this is, we still do not appear to be any closer in ascertaining who exactly Nephthys was. Her image of a woman where the hieroglyphs of her name (a basket and top of a house) made up her headdress appeared on numerous temples. But despite this, epitaphs of her name being recorded as "Mistress of the Gods" and the "Lady of the Body (of the Gods)" and even the meaning of her name being deciphered as "Mistress of the House" or "Mistress of the Mansion" in ancient Egyptian, Nephthys herself remains very much an enigma today.

British Egyptologist Gerald Avery Wainwright suggested that Nephthys was originally a pre-dynastic sky goddess, which could further explain her later joining with Set (originally a storm god) as well as with Min (a fertility and thunderbolt god).[111] Author Lesley Jackson notes that Nephthys was possibly incorporated into the later Osirian and solar myths of Ra because she was either too popular or powerful to ignore, a process seen within other cultures, especially Greek and Roman. Over time, however, Nephthys's status and role declined, especially as the cult of Isis gained in popularity.[112] This may have been the reason for fewer references about Nephthys found within the *Book of Coming Forth by Day*, (more commonly known as the *Egyptian Book of the Dead*) compared with the earlier funerary texts.

If Nephthys was indeed a pre-dynastic deity, then that would explain the absence of larger temples built in her name. Instead, smaller temples have been discovered including one close to or even within a Set temple precinct at Sepermeru (located at modern day Deshasheh, between Heracleopolis and Oxyrhynchus) during the 19th Dynasty of the New Kingdom.

This further linked her with Set.

It was within the Nome VII's district in Upper Egypt that Nephthys was a supreme goddess and reigned as the "first amongst equals". Yet little remains of her worship. She was also referred to as the unique protectress of the sacred bennu bird (Egyptian phoenix), a bird associated with the resurrection, a connection that may have stemmed from Heliopolis, which was renowned for its "House of the Bennu" temple.

The Komir temple near Esna, built during the later Ptolemaic and Roman period, contains a lengthy hymn to Nephthys on its external wall. Believed to have been written by Roman Emperor Antoninus Pius, the goddess was identified as "... the Great, the Most Excellent, dwelling in the Beautiful Country – the abode of Her brother Osiris, Who comes to life again in Her, She who renews for Him the body that once was, in Her name of 'Renewing of Life' ... "[113]. She was also referred to as the "Mistress of Many Festivals ... who love the day of festival, the goddess for whom men and women play the tambourine". Such associations are more commonly associated with the cow goddess, Hathor, and the hymn at Komir interestingly makes no reference whatsoever to Isis, despite other deities being named.

Through being associated with Anuket (a goddess found in the south of Egypt who was responsible for the yearly inundation of the Nile), Nephthys appeared to have been worshipped at Elephantine during the Late Period (712-323 BCE). She was also associated with a number of lion goddesses including Sekhmet, as one chapel within Edfu temple was dedicated to Nephthys. It was at Edfu that a festival known as "The Heart of Nephthys Rejoices" was once held where the liberal consumption of beer was mandated. Reliefs discovered at Denera and Behbert also depicted Nephthys in receipt of beer offerings made by the pharaoh, seemingly strengthening her connection with Sekhmet.

It was the annual rites conducted by the priestesses of Abydos that Nephthys was better known for. These rites enacted the

"Lamentations of Isis and Nephthys" where the priestesses took on the roles of Nephthys and Isis in the mourning the death of Osiris.[114]

Presiding over the funeral rites of the kings, and later the average Egyptians, appeared to be one of the main functions that Nephthys was associated with. English Egyptologist Sir E.A. Wallis Budge interpreted her name as meaning "at the land's end"[115] as referring to the "end of life" or the conclusion of time, the last day of the ancient Egyptian calendar which was when she was born. While this interpretation does not appear to be shared by other scholars, it does connect with Nephthys's role as a funerary goddess. Both the *Pyramid Text* and the *Coffin Text* record Nephthys involved in such rites.

In the *Pyramid Text* Utterance 532, a passage described the recovery of the body of Osiris by Isis and Nephthys who both appeared as birds of prey (in particular, kites, Egyptian hawks, whose piercing cries reminded people of the lamentations that were offered up to the dead) over his funerary bier as they mourned their lost brother. A later Utterance describes Isis as the 'screecher' from the east and Nephthys as the kite from the west, the direction of the land of the dead to the ancient Egyptians. Another Utterance 505 records "Isis is before me and Nephthys is behind me".

As "Mistress of the West" who befriends the deceased, Nephthys offered guidance to the newly departed, as well as comfort to the family of the one who died. Nephthys is the comforter of the dead as the deceased waited for the evening boat of the Sun God Ra to take them into the Underworld. Once in the Underworld, Nephthys would be found standing behind Osiris when the hearts of the deceased were weighed against the feather of Ma'at for divine justice and truth.

As one of the four chief funerary goddesses associated with the sacred art of mummification (the others being Isis Neith and Serqet), Nephthys was the protector of Hapi, one of the four sons of Horus who guarded the embalmed lungs of the deceased. It was therefore Nephthys who delivered the "Breath of Life" to the deceased as indicated in the tomb of Tuthmosis III (Dynasty XVIII) where her epithet was "Nephthys of the Bed of Life". Therefore, whilst Isis represented the life experience, it was Nephthys who proceeded during the traditions into death and beyond.

Being a comforter of the dead led to the belief that Nephthys was a "luminal goddess of the twilight and the in-between places"[116] where she assisted both the gods as well as mortals during the critical times of birth and death. Budge noted that Nephthys also concealed things in that she was reported saying: "I hide the hidden things"[117]·This has been interpreted as implying that the goddess protects by confusion and invisibility as opposed to more direct actions of strength and confrontation. Mead reminds us that "Nephthys is that which is below the earth and non-manifest, while Isis [is] that which is above the earth and manifest."[118]

The *Pyramid Texts* further recorded that Nephthys was "a force before whom demons trembled in fear, and whose magical spells were necessary for navigating the various levels of Duat" (the afterlife). Here, Nephthys escorted the deceased to the west, the land of the dead, where he would face the gods of the Underworld, and, if deemed suitable for rebirth amongst the gods, it was Isis who would then greet him and escort him to the east where the deceased would be reborn.[119]

Nephthys and Isis were the two goddesses of the Hall of Truth known as the Ma'ati, the two birds of prey who appeared at the casket of the dead king, and the two weepers of Osiris. In a land which was itself divided into upper and lower parts, the sisters seemed to encompass everything to the ancient Egyptian people.[120] As mentioned earlier, it was Nephthys who assisted her sister in the recovery of Osiris's dismembered body; it was Isis who retrieved and looked after Anubis when Nephthys was not able to; and even Plutarch described Isis as the "visible" mother for Anubis, the stand-in for Nephthys being the "invisible" yet true mother who "could not be perceived".[121] *Pyramid Text* Utterance 555 also noted that to the deceased, the mother was Isis, whereas the nurse was Nephthys.[122]

From a closer look at both the *Pyramid Text* and the *Coffin Text*, it is clear the Nephthys's main role was that of a funerary goddess. She bound the deceased with her locks of hair before they were able to rise and be transported in the night barge to Osiris's Underworld, being guided by Nephthys who acted as some kind of psychopomp, protecting the deceased through the important journey. Yet this was not her only function. Nephthys was also called upon to protect the king, as with her breath, she was able to annihilate enemies of the king. In doing so, she took on the role of protector of his temple. She further encouraged the pharaoh to overcome his enemies by praising her strength to him. This warrior aspect, coupled with the association with the lion goddesses may have been remnants of a further aspect of Nephthys that has unfortunately been lost to us over the millennia.

## Working with Nephthys

In modern times, the difference between the two sisters can be reflected in how we work with them. Isis is visible, representing birth, growth, development and vigour, whereas Nephthys is invisible, representing death, decay, diminution and immobility. Isis is the magic whereas Nephthys is the mystery. Nephthys is the darkness to Isis's light, the night to her twin sister's day. However, it is important to remember that without the darkness (Nephthys), the light (Isis) would not be.

It is within this "darkness" and the solace which this state brings that the teachings of Nephthys are revealed. As an aspect of the Dark Goddess, she is the protector to those who seek the peace which is brought about from any kind of emotional release, and which teaches the knowledge that can only be found going deep within one's self. Nephthys is also holder of the secrets of ritual as well as the gift of prophecy. For us to become fully aware of her teachings we must find that inner solace of contemplation and inner rest which is partly hidden in the shadows.

On a more personal level, Nephthys is the introvert in an otherwise extraverted pantheon, therefore giving encouragement to introverts that it is fine to retreat to the shadow realms whenever we feel the need, for there is much knowledge and wisdom to be gained from the silent shadows.

Over the millennia the true nature of Nephthys seemed to have been slowly covered with the shifting sands of time as political and religious fashions swayed. As a result, her own individuality had, at least up to a certain point, appeared to have merged with that of her more popular sister. Yet, even in our modern era, stark differences can still be found between the two same-sexed siblings.

Just as the sphinx, once hidden from sight, has now been revealed to show its true beauty, the recent resurgence in the interest surrounding the most silent of the Ennead family could possibly reveal a deeper understanding and indeed appreciation of Nephthys. Yet, it is the shadowy veils that we still must penetrate before her truth is completely revealed. And for any introvert, it is within the echoing silence that the deepest of all mysteries are obtained.

## Invocation to Nephthys

I call to thee, Lady of the House of the Gods,
Guardian of the departed and transformer of magic.
It is you, Nebt-Het, who greets me in the darkness.
Daughter of Nut who shines above
Daughter of Geb who lies beneath me.
It is you, Nebt-Het, whose silence comforts me.
Loyal sister of Osiris and Mistress of the Gods

It is you I call, Protector of the ancient phoenix
Come to me, Nebt-Het, come to me, Nephthys
Grant to me your sacred wisdom.

## Correspondences associated with Nephthys

Kites, eagles, gold, sunsets, twilight, the dark moon, dark blue, purple and black colours, Sirius, myrrh, frankincense, kyphi, amethyst, carnelian, black onyx, lapis lazuli, blue goldstone, orchids, roses, violets.

## Meditation: Meeting the Silent One

Visualise yourself being embraced with the cool swirling mists of time. These mists will take you to another time and place and will also return you to the here and now. With each deep breath, allow the mists of time to permeate your being until you are no longer conscious of the physical realm. You are being transported back in time. Back to a time of the ancient kings of Egypt.

As the mists slowly clear you find yourself standing on the banks of a large river - the River Nile - on the island of Philae, the chief shrine to Isis, the holiest of all holies, before it was relocated when the Aswan dam was built. Take account of your surroundings and what you are wearing. As you do, you become aware of other pilgrims, like yourself, making their way towards the shrine. It is early in the morning with the sun just beginning to rise.

You climb the steps and come to an open court, surrounded by gigantic granite pillars, each one beautifully carved with the various gods of the land. You turn left and enter a colonnade. On each side are two small temples. You stop at one of these small temples to be purified with water and incense, thus making you fit to enter into the Great Temple of Isis.

Continue down the colonnade to a columned hall. The walls and pillars glow with colour, soft and brilliant. The priesthood is gathering to a select number of pilgrims into the inner vestibule that houses the sacred statue of Isis. You hold close to your chest your special offering to the goddess. One of the priesthood motions to you to follow them. They draw back a veil, which conceals a series of steps leading upwards to the inner vestibule.

As you move closer to the inner vestibule, you notice the hieroglyphs on the walls detail prayers and invocations of the goddess, and you can hear the morning prayers being chanted. As the prayers fade you find yourself standing before the sacred statue of Isis. She is more beautiful that you have ever imagined as her robes reflect the colour of the sun's glow, shot with gold and flame. You are overcome with awe of her beauty and as you kneel in front of the statue, you carefully place your offering in front of you.

You become aware of movement in front of you and as you look up, you see emerging from the statue the goddess herself. You are not afraid as her loving presence embraces you. She then draws your attention to your left, where out from the shadows another figure emerges, equally as beautiful, equally as magnificent.

Draped in a cloak of velvety blackness of the midnight sky and scattered with glittering star-like points of light, this figure could be a double of Isis, but she is not. She is Nephthys, the twin sister goddess of Isis, and she speaks to you:

"I am Nephthys - daughter of Geb and Nut
I am Nephthys - sister of Isis and Osiris
I am Nephthys - sister/wife of Set and the mother of Anubis
I am Nephthys - Mistress of the House, the home of the sun
    god Horus
I guide the newly dead and comfort their family
I am the Queen of Magic, of secret knowledge and of prophecy
I am the teacher of religion as well as ritual
I am a Goddess of Ma'at
I am that part of you that guides you, that influences you

That part that threatens you, that makes you feel inadequate,
even ashamed.

I am the darkness to Isis's light

I am death, I am decay and immobility.

Without me, you will never experience the true power of my
sister's strength

Without me, you will never know how to appreciate life

For the two of us must be.

I am there to greet you at the beginning of your life

And although you may forget me,

I wait for you at the end."

Nephthys steps forward and presents you with a gift. This gift
may be an object, a secret password, or a phrase. It may even be
a key to unlock the meaning of future dreams.

You slowly become aware of the continuing prayers of the
priesthood. You are alone in the inner vestibule of the temple.
Your offering is gone - it has been accepted.

Make your way back past the hieroglyphs, down the steps and
through the veil that separates the inner vestibule from the outer
temple. You catch an approving nod from one of the priesthood
as if they know what you have experienced. You move past the
pillars of soft and brilliant colour, through the great pylon and
down the colonnade where the purification temples are housed.
You move past the gigantic granite pillars to the open court.
Descend the steps until you reach the banks of the River Nile.
You notice that the Sun has risen quite considerably from when
you first enter the sacred temple. You feel at peace.

Standing at the river banks, the mists of time begin to swirl
around you for it is time for you to return to the present. The gift
of Nephthys will be with you.

# Ereshkigal: Judge of the Great Below

*Dark sister, my blood, my DNA, my other half,*
*Remind me of all that I am!*
*Messenger from the other worlds that I so crave,*
*calling to me, calling to me...*
*Ground me! Pull me downward, inward,*
*Let me never scorn you, you dear sister goddess who represent*
*all that is hard, all that is besmeared, difficult, ugly,*
*unplanned, unforeseen, all that, deep down, is life itself.*
*Remind me of all that I am.*
*Hold me close within the dark earth, Ereshkigal, close to you.*[123]

As the ruler of the Sumerian Underworld, the Realm of the
Dead, which was known as Irkalla, "the Great Below" or the
"Land of No Return", Ereshkigal was first mentioned in old
Sumerian offering lists. The temples of ki.babbar.e and ki.nam.
tar.ri.da (which were dedicated to her) dated from the period
of the Third Dynasty of Ur, 21st 20th century BCE, this indicates
that she is an extremely ancient goddess, easily predating the
more popular myth of *The Descent of Inanna*.

In the Eridu model[124] of the Sumerian creation myth, Enlil
(Lord Air, Master of Winds) separated Ki (Mother Earth and
Queen) from An (Sky Father and King), causing the primal unity
of heaven and earth to be lost forever. An wept for Ki, longing
for her embrace and kiss, and his tears met Nammu the Sea.
From the mingling of the waters the divine twins, Enki[125] and
Ereshkigal, were born. Enki was the lord of magic, crafts and the
watery deep, the "knowing without" whereas Ereshkigal was
the" knowing within".

When Ereshkigal was kidnapped by Kur (the primeval
Dragon) and taken to his Underworld, Enki built a boat and
descended from the Heights Above to bring her back. It is not

known what actually occurred except that Enki brought back seeds for the future Tree of Knowledge, the Huluppu Tree[126], which he planted along the banks of the Euphrates River, and that Ereshkigal retained the Underworld for her own domain.

In the *Epic of Gilgamesh*, Ereshkigal's husband Gugalanna (the "Bull of Heaven") was sent to earth to battle the hero Gilgamesh, who had refused Inanna's sexual advances. Gugalanna, whose feet were said to have made the earth shake, was slain and dismembered by Gilgamesh and his friend, Enkidu. It was the funeral rites of Gugalanna[127] that Inanna wanted to witness when she was confronted by Neti, the gatekeeper to the Great Below in *The Descent of Inanna*. The Queen of Heaven was constantly reminded that Ereshkigal was the only one who could pass judgement and give laws in her kingdom, and at each of the seven gates, Inanna was made to relinquish an item of status because "the ways of the Underworld are perfect, they may not be questioned.[128]

As with all who trespassed (came uninvited) into her realm, Ereshkigal dealt with Inanna in a similar manner. The Queen of Heaven was stripped of any association with the Land of the Living as well as anything that bore her regal status until she stood naked before the Queen of the Great Below and the Anunnaki, the seven judges of the Underworld. Ereshkigal then "spoke against her the word of wrath and uttered against her the cry of guilt and struck her", and turned Inanna into a corpse which was then hung upon a hook like a piece of rotting meat.

After three days and nights had passed, Inanna's attendant, Ninshubur, reported her absence to Enki, Inanna's father, who created two "galla" (androgynous demons) that went into the Underworld to rescue the Queen of Heaven. Finding Ereshkigal in deep mourning (for a painful and fruitless labour), they sympathized with her, echoing her cries and complaints. Grateful for their attention, Ereshkigal offered them any gift they wanted. They asked for no gift except for Inanna's body, and once in their possession, they restored the Queen of Heaven back to life again with the "Bread of Life" and the "Water of Life". In return for Inanna's release, a substitute had to be found. Inanna refused to allow the demons to take a number of people, including Ninshubur, in exchange for Inanna, as all were dressed in sack cloths and were mourning. When Inanna entered her palace, she found her consort, Dumuzi, not only dressed in his fine garments, but he was also sitting on his throne surrounded by a number of beautiful women. Enraged by what she saw, Inanna instructs the demons to take Dumuzi into the Great Below in her palace.

When these two myths (*Epic of Gilgamesh* and *Descent of Inanna*) are looked together, we gain a better understanding as to why Ereshkigal treated Inanna in such a way – it was because of Inanna that Ereshkigal's husband was killed. Ereshkigal's "word of wrath" and the "cry of guilt" against Inanna makes more sense, as does her moaning when the galla found her – she mourning the loss of her husband Gugalanna.

What is interestingly omitted from the modern interpretations of the *Descent of Inanna* are the very last few lines of the poem where Ereshkigal is praised, not Inanna.

Modern interpretations often allude to the fact Inanna's treatment was based on jealousy of her sexual exploitations. Such interpretations seem to overlook any connection between Ereshkigal and Gugalanna as well as fragmented cuneiform script, possibly from the later Babylonian period, that mention Ereshkigal having a second (and somewhat younger) husband, Nergal, the stubborn God of War and Pestilence.

Of the two different versions of the Ereshkigal and Nergal myth, the earlier one, found at Tell El-Amarna in Egypt, dated from 15th or 14th century BCE, is considered to be incomplete as it consisted of only 90 lines. The much later 7th century BCE (late Assyrian version from Sultantepe) consisted of some 750 lines. Assyriologists tend to perceive the myth as Ereshkigal's surrender to Nergal, relinquishing her sole authority over the Realm of the Dead to a male god, whereas other interpretations are that Ereshkigal gave up separateness in order to be fulfilled by the beloved's essence without losing sight of her own uniqueness.[129]

In this myth, An (Sky Father) sent a message to the Great Below for Ereshkigal to attend a grand banquet in order to keep the balance between life and death, darkness and light, chaos and order. According to cosmic regulations, the gods of the upper world could not descend into the Underworld, nor could the chthonic deities ascend to the heavens. As such, as she could not leave her realm, Ereshkigal sent her trusted vizier Namtar to be her representative before whom all the gods bowed and showed respect, except for the young god Nergal. When it was demanded that he had should show respect to Namtar, Nergal stated that as he had never met Ereshkigal, he would not show respect to her or anyone attending as her representative. This action was perceived as one of great offence and Nergal was ordered to descend into the Great Below and beg Ereshkigal for forgiveness.

Before he departed, Enki the Wise warned the young god not to eat or drink anything, not to wash his feet and, most importantly, not to "do that which men and woman do".

Having passed through the seven gates, the sight of Ereshkigal caught Nergal by surprised as she was not the old hag he had expected to meet. Instead, she was so beautiful that the young god forgot the warning Enki had given him. It was not until some seven days had passed that Nergal returned to the Land Above. However, he did so without letting Ereshkigal know, and was only seen by Namtar, Ereshkigal's messenger. When the queen was notified of her lover's departure, she threatened to raise the dead until they outnumbered the living if the other gods did not send Nergal back. And return he did, where together they ruled.[130]

## Working with Ereshkigal

As a Dark Goddess, Ereshkigal represents a number of things including depression and the agony of helplessness, unaccountable desire and transformative destructive energy, as well as unacceptable autonomy (the need for separate-ness and self-assertion)[131]. She is considered to be the goddess who looks after what has been discarded and no longer wanted, as well as the rubbish etc. Being the "Mistress of Essence", Ereshkigal also teaches us to go beyond appearances, to the reality of justice and truth. Needless to say, these can be immensely difficult thresholds to cross over in everyday life.

*The Descent of Inanna* is probably one of the more popular myths used when working with the Dark Goddess, or even when addressing the shadow aspects of the Self due to the process of having to move through the seven gates. These gates are often used as important markers for people who are wishing to explore the Underworld because we are to leave specific aspects of our personality or identity, each of which reveals or exposes a deeper level of our own authentic self.

When looking at *The Descent of Inanna* there is one important aspect that is often overlooked, and that is that Ereshkigal was the one who held the power to release the Radiant One (Inanna) and because of this she should not be ignored. It is she, the lady of the Great Below that gives the myth focus, motivation and even resolution to Inanna's descent and subsequent rise back to the surface. Ereshkigal further reminds us how important it is that we balance the light (Inanna) and dark (Ereshkigal) within our own selves

## Invocation to Ereshkigal

I call to thee, the great Ereshkigal
Lady of Irkalla and of the eternal darkness
Widow of Gugalanna, the Great Bull of Heaven,
Beloved of Nergal, the Ruler of Pestilence.

It is you who drinks with the Anunnaki, eating the dust and
   clay for bread
It is you who weeps for those abandoned by love.
It is you who mourns those expelled before their time.
It is you, great Mistress of the Seven Gates, who I call.
I hail you in your sorrow as you hail me in mine.
It is you who holds the water-gift, the river in its fullness.
It is you who holds the grain-gift, the fields in their fullness.
It is you who taught the Queen of Heaven in her arrogance.
I ask you to teach me in mine.
Humble I stand before you, Lady of Irkalla
Teach me the wisdom of the kurgarra and galatur.
Enable me to move beyond myself and my fears.
I call to thee, mighty Ereshkigal,
Grant to me your sacred wisdom.

## Correspondences associated with Ereshkigal
Bull, skulls, lions, ziggurat, doors/gates, the dark moon, dirt,
purple, deep blue and black colours, lapis lazuli, blue goldstone,
black obsidian, rosemary, bay laurel.

## Meditation: Journey to the Great Below
You find yourself standing before the first gate to the Underworld,
the Great Below. Its gatekeeper, Neti, advises that in order for
you to enter, you need to vibrate the sacred word for that is
the key to opening the gate and which will enable you to step
beyond into the Great Below. It is at this first gate, the sahasrara,
or crown, chakra, where Inanna relinquished her own crown,
her godhood. Inhale and intone: EEEAAA.

   The gates slowly open. There is a path winding through the
darkness to the right, widdershins in the Southern Hemisphere,
the direction against the sun[132]. Neti takes one of the torches from
the wall and you follow him through the gateway and down
along the winding path. It is not long before you come to the

second gate to the Underworld. This gate relates to the ajna, or third eye, chakra, and is where Inanna relinquished her necklace which represented her charisma and glamour, her magic and ability to manifest. You inhale and intone the key for this gate: REEEE.

The gates open and you step through guided by Neti. Downward, winding to the right, you walk until you come to the third gate to the Great Below. At this gate, the vishuddha, or throat, chakra, Inanna relinquished two oval stones that represented her birthing ability, her femininity and fertility. You inhale and intone the key for this gate: IIISSSHHH.

Once again, the gates slowly open, you step through guided by Neti. You continue walking downward until you come to the fourth gate that represents that anahata, or heart, chakra. It was at this gate that Inanna relinquished her breastplate called "Come, man, come" that represented her sexual allure and emotional heart. Inhale and intone KKKAAA.

The gates open, you step through with Neti by your side and continue walking downwards, winding to the right. You come to the fifth gate which relates to the manipura, or solar plexus, chakra. Here Inanna relinquished her golden hip girdle that represented her ego and sacred seal. Inhale and intone the key for this gate: HHHAAA.

The gates open, you step through with Neti by your side and continue walking downwards, winding to the right. You come to the sixth gate which relates to the svadhisthana, or sacral, chakra, where Inanna relinquished her lapis measuring rod and line in her hand that represented her will and authority. Inhale and intone the key for this gate: HHHAAA.

The gates open, you step through with Neti by your side and continue walking downwards, winding to the right. You come to the seventh gate, the final to the Great Below. This gate is very imposing, highly decorated with magnificent carvings. At this gate, the muladhara, or base chakra, is where Inanna relinquished her garment of ladyship, the breechcloth that represented her robe of deity. Inhale and intone the key for this gate: EEEELLLLL

The gate slowly opens and you step into a courtyard decorated with lapis lazuli tiles offset with opalescent moonstone. Namtar, the vizier of the Great Below, approaches and takes your torch. "There is no need for the light from above here," he says as the torch is extinguished and placed in a bracket by the gate.

Before you is a throne made from polished black obsidian, and sitting upon it is a dark-haired woman who is neither young nor old, neither beautiful nor plain. She beckons you closer and you notice a veil covers part of her face. She speaks:

"I am Ereshkigal, the ruler of the Great Below, the realm of the forgotten and the unwanted, the ignored and neglected. I take what does not shine in the light and return to it life and acceptance, for everything has its own beauty. Inanna calls for beauty and purification, for in the light it is the surface that is seen and judged by others according to their perceptions. There is no place for such illusions and fantasies here, for I see the beauty that is hidden, that is not always obvious, that lies below the surface, hidden deep within your soul.

Bring me your tears, your sorrow, your anxiety and fears. Cry with me your tears formed through pain and loneliness. Moan with me your anguish and disappointment. Strip away the illusion and falsities for they have no place here in the Great Below. Bare naked your soul, expose your true self. Look deep within yourself, behind the masks that you wear. Expose that true self you hide, that you are ashamed off, that you try to ignore. Come and cry with me."

You breathe in your darkness, the sorrow, loneliness and despair. As you do, feel these emotions sinking down through your body like lead in water. As you exhale, feel these emotions sink down through your muladhara (base) chakra into the earth. With each release of darkness, the following inhalation becomes a little lighter. Continue breathing until you are breathing in the lightness. When you inhale complete lightness, you are cleansed and blessed by Ereshkigal.

The Queen of the Great Below smiles at you and disappears before your eyes. Namtar is waiting with your torch, the light from above has been relit. As you start your ascent to the surface back through the seven gates, you are moving now to the left[133], with the sun in the Southern Hemisphere.

# Hel: Norse Goddess of the Dead

*Now Loki comes, cause of all ill!*
*Men and Æsir curse him still.*
*Long shall the gods deplore,*
*Even till Time be o'er,*
*His base fraud on Asgard's hill.*
*While, deep in Jotunheim, most fell,*
*Are Fenrir, Serpent, and Dread Hel,*
*Pain, Sin, and Death, his children three,*
*Brought up and cherished; thro' them he*
*Tormentor of the world shall be.*[134]

As far back as the 9th century, Hel (also known as Hela) was mentioned in Nordic poetry. Within the *Heimskringla* and later in the 10th century *Egil's Saga*, as well as the more popular works from the 13th century, being the *Poetic Edda* (compiled from earlier traditional sources) and the *Prose Edda*[135], Hel was mentioned as being the ruler of the Nordic Underworld that also bore her name. When a Nordic person died, they "went to Hel".

The *Prose Edda* described Hel as being half alive and half dead, with a "gloomy down-cast appearance" and the bones on one side of her face exposed. With the wave of her hand, Hel is able to cause death, decay and disease. When the Black Death epidemic of the Middle Ages depopulated villages across Scandinavia, it was Hel who was considered responsible for having left her dismal abode to ride about the land on her broom (or a three-legged white horse) spreading the bubonic plague.

This connection with death is further evidenced in the etymology of the Norse goddess's name. According to Maria Kvilhaug[136], the word "Hel" is derived from *helja* (meaning "to hide"), *helu*, ("cold" or "frost"), and *hella*, ("stone", in particular large, flat, over hanging stones or rocks that occur over cliffs or caves). Aside from death, these words also indicate a connection with nature. Another name linked with Hel is that of Huldra, who was considered to be a queen of people who lived underground or within a mountain, or a spirit that dwells in the forest.

In the 9th century poem, *Ynglingatal*, Hel was described as the goddess of Glitnir who took "lustful pleasure in the corpse of Dyggvi", a king. It is interesting to note that *glitnir* means "glittering", alluding to the possibility that Hel was "the goddess of a glittering place". It is also worth noting that all the Norse gods will dwell with Hel after Ragnarok (the end of the world). The aforementioned *Prose Edda* was written much later, after Christianity had arrived in Scandinavia. This affected how Hel and her realm were depicted. According to Kvilhaug, several examples of Skaldic poetry described Hel as being an attractive maiden. This appeared to contradict the depiction found within the *Prose Edda* where she was described as being half black and half white with a perpetually grim and fierce expression on her face. Hel was also considered to be rather greedy, harsh and even cruel, or at least indifferent to the concerns of the living as well as the dead.

Kvilhaug associates Hel with the word *helgi*, meaning "sacred" which is closely related to the Norwegian *hele* meaning "to heal" or it may have come from the Old Norse meaning "hidden" which may relate to the Underworld as well as the dead being "hidden" or buried in the ground. When these other associations are taken into account, it would appear that Hel is not simply a goddess of death, but she is also a goddess of healing, and it is recorded within the sagas that her realm, Helheim, was a place that was sought out by gods and heroes alike.

It is within Sturluson's recording of the *Prose Edda*[137] that the story of "Gylfaginning" can be found that relates to the creation of the world, and indicates that it was the union of the trickster god Loki and a female giantess, Angrboda (herald of sorrows) that resulted with the birth of Hel, the wolf Fenrir (who could destroy Asgard, the home of the gods, during Ragnarok, the end of the cosmos), and Jömungandr, the serpent who lay at the bottom of the ocean wrapped around the world with his tail in his mouth (as he held the world together). The Norse gods "traced prophecies, "that from these siblings great mischief and disaster would arise for them"[138], which was partially due to the nature of their father, Loki, the Norse trickster. Odin provided Hel with her own realm, located in Niflheim (Helheim), (the "abode of mist"). Here she held authority over the nine worlds that were unified by the world tree, Yggdrasil. In exchange, Hel gifted Odin two ravens, Huginn (thought) and Muninn (memory), who acted as the messengers between this world and the next, opening the pathways to death's own realm.

As the ruler of Niflheim, Hel had to "administer board and lodgings to those sent to her, that is, those who die of sickness or old age"[139]. She was the judge who determined the fate of each soul that entered the Afterlife. To the "evil dead", she banished them to the torturous realms of icy cold (a fate considered by the Nordic people to be worse than a lake of fire). Unlike the later Judeo-Christian perception of "Hell", Niflheim was also seen as a place of shelter and gathering for souls that were about to incarnate. Hel watched over those souls who did not choose the path of war and violence, and who died peacefully of old age or illness, as well as women and children who died in childbirth. This latter concept has seen Hel become identified as a guardian for children.

One of Hel's key roles also included the attempted resurrection of Odin's second son, Baldr, who died after being tricked into taking part in a competition that was rigged by Loki, Hel's own father. According to the *Gesta Danorum* (accredited as being written by Danish historian Saxo Grammaticus in the 13th century), Baldr had a prophetic dream whereby the ancient Roman Proserpina (interpreted by Grammaticus as the "Goddess of Death") stood by his side and informed him that she would clasp him in her arms in three days' time. Upon hearing this, Frigg, Baldr's mother, made every object on earth vow that it would never hurt her son. The only exception was the mistletoe which Frigg had thought was unimportant and non-threatening, or too young to undertake such an oath. Upon discovering this oversight, Loki fashioned either an arrow (or a spear) from the plant. Three days later, during a game the Gods were playing that involved hurling objects at Baldr that harmlessly bounced off him, Loki gave the newly fashioned arrow (spear) to Baldr's brother, the blind god Höðr, to throw. Instead of causing no injury, the mistletoe arrow (spear) inadvertently killed Baldr. Odin and the giantess Rindr then conceived Vali (who grew into manhood within a day), and who then slew Höðr.

Baldr's arrival at Hel's realm was marked by a banquet and festival. His presence, however, was so missed by the other gods that Frigg called for a volunteer to enter Hel's realm and offer the fearful goddess a ransom in exchange for Baldr. The reward of such an heroic deed would be "all her love and favour"[140]. Hermóðr the Brave ("war spirit") undertook this task and upon his arrival at Niflheim, begged Hel to release Baldr as a great weeping had occurred throughout Asgard since his death.[141] In response, Hel indicated that this love for Baldr that Hermóðr claimed had to be tested as "if all things in the world, alive or dead, weep for him, then he will be allowed to return to the Æsir. If anyone speaks against him or refuses to cry, then he will remain with Hel."[142]

When the giantess Pökk refused to weep over Baldr's death and declared that Hel should "hold what she has"[143], the other gods considered that she was actually Loki in disguise. Her refusal to shed a tear ensured Baldr remained in Niflheim and it would be only until after Ragnarök that he would be reconciled with Höðr, whereby the two brothers would rule the new earth along with Thor's sons.

The Nordic shamans, the Seidhr, are believed to call upon

Hel for her protection when they put on the *helkappe*, a magic mask that renders them invisible and enables them to pass through the gateway into the realm of death and spirit. Hel is also associated with the runic symbol *Hagalaz* (meaning "hailstone" or "destruction") which refers to a change through crisis or having past patterns confronted. Often considered to contain negative attributes such as losing power or property, or even obsession with the past, the Hagalaz rune (which signifies change, disruption as well as manifestation) can also shock the person into the "reality of things" as opposed to a continuation of rose-tinted perceptions. At times it is only through experiencing the ill effects of one's own accountability that opens to a deeper spiritual awakening and profound unconscious exploration.

## Working with Hel

Similar to other Dark Goddesses, Hel's arrival in our life may cause initial discomfort and at times, even deep emotional pain. However, when we emerge at the end of the tunnel, we find ourselves permanently transformed and spiritually alive.

## Invocation to Hel

Hail to you, Hel, the Queen of Helheim
The wisest of wights and guardian of souls.
It is you I honour, who feeds the dead
Without fame or fortune, wealth or status.
It is you I honour, embracing life and death
The gift that is beyond physical gain.
It is you I honour, who praises loss and death
The mystery of the passing of all things
For there is no place for pride or ego
At your sacred table
And death is the great leveller
Within your sacred hall.

Hail to you, Hel, the Queen of Helheim
Keeper of the sacredness beyond this world.

## Correspondences associated with Hel

Skulls, serpent, wolf, goose, raven, dog, Hagalaz rune, black and white colours, apples, hail, ice, snow, jasmine, juniper berries, white willow bark, cedar, myrrh, storax, black agate, lead, obsidian, onyx.

## Meditation: Revealing Your True Self

You find yourself in a clearing covered in pine needles from the surrounding pine trees that have been so closely planted together sunlight barely enters. Yet you feel protected and safe within this clearing. The branches gently sway in the breeze and out of the corner of your eye something catches your attention. You feel some kind of presence and depth amongst the shadows. Feeling drawn, you make your way to the edge of the clearing where there appears to be an energetic portal. The closer you move to this portal, the more the branches of the trees sway, yet you feel no wind on your skin. Only an otherworldly presence.

A shift in shadows and then you see her. In the dancing branches, a beautiful young woman appears before disappearing from view, leaving only the pine boughs and twigs in sight, only to reappear again. This time standing right before you.

You gasp for the right side of her face appears to be almost completely rotted off. Bone, sinew, and dark caverns are exposed where flesh should have been. By contrast, the left side of her face has clear, ivory skin covering a high cheekbone. She does not speak, only gazes at you with her perfect left eye. Her right eye is a vacant socket.

No words are spoken yet her presence is vast and commanding. She waits, staring silently at you, straightening her dark grey shift from time to time; waiting to see what you will do. Will you speak? Does her exposed half face revolt you?

Despite her macabre appearance, you do not feel afraid. You know that with her deathly face that she can only be Lady Death. There is something familiar about her, yet you cannot put your finger on it. All you do know is that there is a sense of power emanating from her. Then you realise that this power is a reflection of your own inner darkness and she is but a mirror.

She moves closer and your heart quickens a beat. Her hand reaches to gently touch your cheek and as it does, you feel love emanate from her. You close your eyes, surrendering to her touch, her presence. Instinctively you know her name although nothing has been spoken. She is Hel, the daughter of Loki, the ruler of Helheim, where the souls of those who were slain in battle go.

The touch of her hand against your skin makes you shiver and then shake. As your body shakes you feel as if outer aspects of yourself are beginning to shed. These are the aspects that you have attained through attempting to live up to other people's expectations, or even what you have felt other people expected you to do or think or even feel. The more your body shakes and shivers with the touch of Hel's hands, the more layers fall away until what is exposed it your true authentic self. The person who your soul is to be in this incarnation.

You open your eyes and see Hel staring at your intensely. As you return her gaze, focusing on her one good eye, you see a symbol beginning to form in your mind's eye. It is like the letter "H" and you realise that it is that of Hagalaz, the rune which means change, disruption, and also manifestation.

You know that in order to be your true authentic self you will need to change. Change is always disruptive and means making adjustments. Often it is the change itself that people fear, as opposed to the inability to control what will change and when it will change. As we change, not everyone around us is able to adjust. Our ability and willingness to accept change, highlights their inability. This in turn can result in people once close to us

# Baba Yaga: The Slavic Initiator

*Mother Goddess, show me the secrets of my heart.*
*Show me where I have wandered off my path.*
*Show me how to find my path again.*
*Fly before me, illuminating my path.*
*Fly before me, showing me the broad road.*
*Into my best future, show me the way*
*Prepare the way for my searching feet*
*O Mother of Light, you who dwell in the South*
*On nine wooded hills, O show me the way.*
(Siberian Shaman Prayer )[144]

The Slavic goddess Baba Yaga's name shows a contradicting duality where *Baba* means "grandmother" or "wise old woman" and *yaga* "horror", "evil woman" or "witch". She is the giver of gifts or adulthood; yet she is also the bringer of death. She is considered to be the grand crone, the goddess of wisdom and death, the Bone Mother. Wild and untameable, she is also the nature spirit bringing wisdom and death of ego, and through death, rebirth. In fairy tales, Baba Yaga is an old hag with long grey hair and sharp teeth, who flies through the air in her mortar while using the pestle as a paddle.

Located deep in the forest, her hut stands on a pair of chicken legs, with human feet as bolts and human hands as hinges. It is surrounded by a fence of human bones that are topped with human skulls with eyes illuminating the darkness. Any visitor who enters her hut is asked whether they came of their own free will, or whether they were sent. It is within the Slavic tale of *Vasilissa the Beautiful*[145] that we meet Baba Yaga.

When Vasilissa was about eight years old, her mother died and just prior to her death, she gave the girl a tiny wooden doll, advising her that she should always carry the doll in her pocket.

Should evil threaten or sorrow befall upon her, all Vasilissa was to do was to give the doll something to eat and drink and it would advise how she should act during times of need.

After her mother died, eventually Vasilissa's father remarried. However, this woman was cold and cruel, having only married the merchant for his money. Her two daughters were equally as cruel, and all three set about instructing Vasilissa to undertake difficult tasks that she was only able to complete with the help of her doll.

One day the merchant had to travel to a distant kingdom and before he was scarcely out of sight, the stepmother sold the house and moved the family into a gloomy one on the edge of the forest. Each day the stepmother sent Vasilissa into the forest in the hope that she would encounter Baba Yaga who was said to eat children. However, each evening Vasilissa made it back home.

One day the stepmother put out all the fires in the house and Vasilissa was sent to fetch light from Baba Yaga's hut. As she set out on her journey, a mysterious man rode by Vasilissa, dressed in white, riding a white horse whose harness was also white. As she continued to walk, a similar rider passed her, except he was clad all in red and on a blood red horse. Eventually she came to a house that stood on chicken legs and was surrounded by a fence made from human bones. A third rider, like the others, but dressed in black and on a coal black horse rode past her. As he passed her, the night fell, and the eye sockets of the skulls became luminous. Vasilissa was too frightened to run away, and so Baba Yaga found her when she arrived in her mortar.

Telling the witch that her stepmother had sent her to borrow some fire, Vasilissa was set to work to earn the fire, or be eaten for supper. The first task was that Vasilissa had to clean the house and yard, cook supper, and pick the mouldy corn out from the good grain. After Baba Yaga left, Vasilissa set about cooking the meal while her doll attended to the other chores. At dawn, the white rider passed; at or before noon, the red. As the black rider rode past, Baba Yaga returned, bade three pairs of disembodied hands to grind the corn, and set Vasilissa the same tasks for the next day, with the addition of sorting out black grains from wild peas. Again, the doll did all except cooking the meal. Upon her return, Baba Yaga again set the three pairs of hands to grind the grain. The tasks for the third day were also very similar and included cleaning poppy seeds that had been mixed with dirt.

While undertaking the tasks, Vasilissa remained silent until Baba Yaga asked her if she was dumb, and told the girl that she could ask a question. Vasilissa asked about the three riders, to which she was told that they were servants of Baba Yaga. The white was her "bright day", the red was the "round sun" and the black one was the night. In return, Baba Yaga demanded the cause of Vasilissa's success with respect to the tasks that were set. On hearing the answer "by my mother's blessing", Baba Yaga sent Vasilissa home as she did not want "one who bears a blessing" to cross her threshold. Before the girl got to the gate, Baba Yaga flung a skull with burning eyes at her and said that this was the fire that Vasilissa's stepmother had requested.

Upon her return, the light from the skull burnt the stepmother and Vasilissa's stepsisters to ashes. Vasilissa moved back to the village where she was taken in by an old woman, all the time feeding her little doll. One day, the Tsar bought a piece of linen that Vasilissa had woven and requested her presence. Upon seeing her beauty, the Tsar married Vasilissa and together with the old woman, Vasilissa went to live in the palace, with her wooden doll in her pocket.

In folklore and myth, Baba Yaga is portrayed as both the antagonist and the guide. As an aspect of the Dark Goddess, she is wise, and gives gifts of splendour to the worthy, but most often she is the Bone Mother, the devourer of human flesh. Her home is built from the bones of her victims, and in many tales, she is said to kidnap children to eat for supper. This aspect of her character, though terrible at first glance, can be seen as a guiding principle, as well as a doorway to initiation.

The accepting the mystery of the unknown is where Baba Yaga teaches us to release the tameness of life and step out into the wild, the forests, and seek adventures. To embrace wildness is an exercise which leads to freedom of spirit and ego. Within our untamed, uncivilized Self, there are no restrictions, no buckling to fear, and no illusions. Our wild spirit is where we find the creative power to build our own path, our own destinies, and change the world around us.

Baba Yaga's only request to the traveller who enters her home of darkness is that they do so of their own free will. Once inside, completion of the tasks she requests earns the practitioner great rewards.

## Working with Baba Yaga

When working with Baba Yaga she places you in situations that test your intuition, that wash away the innocence of youth so that you can learn to trust your adult self. In this manner, adolescence is not measured by age, but rather by experience. She devours innocence and naivety, peels back the skin in order to eat the flesh of ignorance and illusion, to leave the bones of your true self exposed. As the innocence dies, the experiences and temperament of those past times remains; in her role as life/ death/rebirth, Baba Yaga is simply "killing" the parts of your mind and life which are no longer of consequence, to make way for the new. She then gives you the nourishment you need in the form of wisdom-gaining experiences.

Baba Yaga teaches us about the unconscious mind, and the effect it has on our lives even when we are not paying attention. Under her instruction we discover the strength of our intuition and learn to trust it regardless of what our friends, family or even logic says. Once we learn to trust our instincts and follow our intuition, we are, in a sense, no longer a part of the world –

we walk between the worlds.

## Invocation to Baba Yaga

I call to thee, Great Grandmother
She who is wild, untamed and unapologetic
Deep in your forest of birch
At the end of the world I seek thee.
You who are propelled by creation and destruction.
With your mighty broom you sweep from this world
That which is no longer needed
Teach me the ways of releasing and drawing.
Show me the beauty of living and dying.
Instil upon me the importance of strength and yielding.
Bravely I stand before your hut and face the door,
I know, Great Grandmother, it is within your oven
That lies the secret of death and rebirth.
I offer my soul, Baba Yaga, to be reborn.
May we rise together above the forest.
Grant me safe passage in your sacred mortar.

## Correspondences associated with Baba Yaga

Skulls, chicken, lantern, cat, snake, broom, mortar and pestle, birch, white, red and black colours, garnet, bloodstone, tourmaline, smoky quartz sandalwood, geranium, patchouli.

## Meditation: Transformation of the Self

You find yourself walking along a path that runs deep within a forest, the trees are so old and thick that sunlight can barely penetrate. You soon come to a clearing and in the middle is an unusual looking house, built on what looks like stilts. Around the house is a fence made from bones and skulls. You realise that this is the home of Baba Yaga, the Slavic grandmotherly witch of the forest. Push open the gate and walk up the path.

The door to the house swings open and standing before you

is a wizened old lady, her grey hair is covered with a scarf and she wears an apron tied around her waist. She eyes you up and down, mutters something under her breath and turns to shuffle back inside her house. For a moment you wonder whether you are to follow her then she commands: "Well, don't stand there, child, I've been waiting for you, the kettle's about to boil." As if on cue, you hear a faint whistle, and tentatively follow the old woman inside.

Your eyes adjust to the half-light of her cottage, taking in the clutter of shelves overflowing with bottles, boxes and other objects, and bunches of herbs hanging from the ceiling to dry. Dominating the room is one of the largest hearths you have ever seen. Baba Yaga motions for you to pour water from the kettle into the cups waiting on the hearth. The air is filled with fragrant herbs and you are dying to ask what they are, but don't. Handing one of the cups to this aged old woman, you sit opposite her.

Settling back in an overstuffed chair, Baba Yaga lets out a sigh. "You come here seeking answers - but do you really want to know the truth? For the truth I will tell you could very well turn your world upside down. It cannot be written about. And those who write the books merely pretend that they know the truth – few of them actually do though. But then it is up to you whether you want to listen to an old mad woman or not."

She closes her eyes as if to allow a smile creep across her face. Then suddenly her eyes are alert and staring at you intensely. "Why aren't you finding your own truth?" she demands. "Why do you listen to the words of fools? Is that why you are here? You've forgotten who you are? You've forgotten your truth?" Her tone is accusing and you feel as if she has smacked you with a wooden spoon for doing something wrong. You struggle to understand what she is talking about as your head starts to swim, and your sight becomes blurry. Amongst the confusion you hear her laugh. Was there something else in the tea? Have you been poisoned by this old woman who lives alone in the forest?

You feel her breath on your face as she leans closer towards you. "The truth can only be experienced, child. Don't fight it – experience it. Learn the Mysteries for yourself." You breathe deeply and prepare yourself to surrender to the experience. As soon as you decide to stop fighting, the sensations dissipate. You cautiously open one eye, then the other, only to find Baba Yaga poking a log in the hearth with a poker, muttering to herself: "Knowledge comes from within. Yet people are constantly looking towards the stars, looking at the world outside of themselves as opposed to within." She encases the fire with a guard and stares at your intensely. "It's late and there is much to do. We need to fly."

You follow her outside to where her mortar is, and suddenly the two of you are flying over the canopy of the forest. As the treetops scrape the bottom of the mortar, Baba Yaga cackles, her sharp iron teeth glinting in the fading light. Below you, what seem to be images of your life pass and in the distance you see a camp fire. Your instinctively know that it is towards this fire that you are heading.

The mortar lands and Baba Yaga guides you to the fire. She thrusts a piece of parchment and ink pen into your hands. "Write," she instructs. "Write what you want to be. Write what you need to release. Write it all." Without any prompting the pen starts to move across the parchment. The writing is in your own handwriting yet you are not moving the pen. Before long the parchment is covered with your dreams and desires, your fears and phobias. Instinctively you screw up the parchment and throw it into the fire. As you do, Baba Yaga cackles and begins to dance around the fire wildly. With a sense of freedom or delusion, you join her in her wild dance. Around and around the fire you dance, cackling with Baba Yaga.

As the fire dies the dancing ceases and you realise that you are alone. There is no sign of Baba Yaga or her mortar. Only a lantern next to the fire. Holding the lantern, you notice a path between the trees and know that this will take you back through the forest. As you walk, you know that something has happened to you – in the cottage, around the fire. You may not know exactly what or how, but with each step you feel transformed.

Hekate by Soror Basilisk

# Rising from the Underworld

Prior to Inanna descending into the Underworld, the Queen of Heaven instructs her faithful handmaiden, Ninshubur, on what to do if she fails to return at the expected time. When this occurs, Ninshubur goes to the three gods Inanna had instructed her to seek. Only Enki, the God of Wisdom, agrees to assist as both Enlil (God of the Air) and Nanna (God of the Moon) thought Inanna had ventured too far. From the dirt underneath his fingernails, Enki fashions two creatures, Galatur and Kurgarra, who are able to slip under the Underworld gates undetected and gain entry into Ereshkigal's realm. Here they find the Queen of the Great Below moaning with labour pains. Each time she moans the creatures moan with her. This appeases Ereshkigal, as up until now she has not received any empathy or compassion (probably Inanna's greatest mistake was that she failed to ask the Queen of the Great Below what ailed her).

Having received empathy and compassion from these creatures, Ereshkigal expresses her gratitude by asking the two creatures what their wishes are. The creatures refuse anything for their own gain, but ask for Inanna's corpse. Ereshkigal concedes and they sprinkle Inanna's body with water and the food of life, enabling Inanna to be reborn.

Wishing to leave the Underworld, Inanna is advised that no one ascends unmarked. As a part of the Queen of Heaven must remain to ensure that a passageway between the Upper World, the Great Above, and the Great Below is kept open. Inanna needs to find a suitable person to take her place in the Underworld.

Followed by Underworld demons, Inanna returns to her Upper World kingdom in search of a suitable person to be exchanged. Each time the demons attempt to take one of Inanna's followers the goddess stops them because the follower is mourning for her death. It is not until Inanna returns to her palace that she hears the sounds of laughter and Inanna finds that her consort Dumuzi is not only sitting on her throne but appears to be hosting some kind of party. Infuriated by his lack of mourning, Inanna nominates him to be her replacement in the Great Below. As the demons seize Dumuzi he prays to Utu, the Sun God, to save him, and is turned into a snake but is captured and brought into the Underworld. His sister, Geshtinanna, volunteers to be a substitute for Dumuzi, and it was decided that they would each spend half the year in the Underworld.

After spending three days and three nights in the Underworld, Inanna is able to see situations (i.e. her relationship with Dumuzi) from a different perspective upon her return. This provides her with the ability to reassess what is important in her life. It is interesting to note that Ereshkigal's husband, Gugalanna, whose death she was mourning, was caused by Inanna, and in the end, Inanna offered up her own partner, Dumuzi. Was this action an attempt to heal the great sorrow that she had caused?

Our return from the Great Below is just as important as our descent. In some circumstances being able to reintegrate fully into the Upper World can take much longer and the transition is not always easy. We have changed, even if we may not know it yet, and the change continues. This is because right from the beginning we made an unconscious effort to descend in the first place.

Often, we find ourselves in situations or positions after our ascent where returning to our previous life is impossible. Our interests have changed, our responsibilities have changed, what we consider important has changed. Life after our ascent, when we find more and more layers being stripped away can be confusing and the more we attempt to hang on to the past, the more we can feel out of control.

It is not uncommon for relationships to crumble and dissolve around you, often without reason, and there is nothing that you can do about it. It may even be the way you view your relationships because your descent and time spent in the Underworld may have changed your perception on what is actually important to you. You are simply not the same person you were prior to the journey, especially if the descent was involuntary. How could anyone remain the same after such a journey? Yet often people resist change and the person you are becoming after journeying with the Dark Goddess can be extremely confronting for other people in your life. Often your journey and subsequent change reflects like a mirror, especially if it relates to health, being a sharp reminder of all limitations of the mental and physical self.

Sometimes we emerge from our Underworld descent half expecting those we care about to be waiting for us with bated breath. Instead we often arise alone and when we see our nearest and dearest they are like Dumuzi, carrying on with their own lives which they have not put on hold for us. And often it is extremely difficult to return to being that post-journey person, even if we want to.

Despite the emotional and even physical pain, destruction and dissolution of a previous existence the true realisation of the actual role of the Dark Goddess in our lives often only comes after our ascent, our rise back to the surface and our subsequent attempt of integration back into "normal" society. From personal experience I have found that I keep turning to meditation, in particular the practice of japa (where a divine name or mantra is repeated using mala or prayer beads), in order to assist with easing into my ongoing soul transitions and to gain a degree of clarity to enable me to continue with every day existence.

At the end of the day it is all about balance. Our modern world seems to be obsessed with happiness, light, and positivity, that to descend into the darkness, to be sad, to be unhappy, is to say that there is something wrong with you, or that you have failed. To keep up the illusion of perpetual happiness mood altering (or suppressing) drugs are on the increase. So too is suicide and depression.

The judges of the Underworld, the Anunnaki, are aspects of us that hold others (or self) in contempt, in criticism, ridiculing, humiliating, bullying, betraying. It is the part of us that sees through our own self-deception, our own lies. They are also the aspects of self that will no longer tolerate our lies, sabotage, small games, self-destruction.

The Dark Goddess is about change, either voluntary or forced (from a soul level), whether it is from moving from childhood through teenage years into adulthood, undergoing rites of passage (including childbirth and parenthood), and especially, as in my case, serious illness. It is she who initiates us into the next stage, our next role or level of soul evolution.

Kali by Soror Basilisk

# Part III

# Working with the Dark Goddess

# Ode to Hel

(Frances Billinghurst, 2019)

Hail to thee, Hel, O Queen of Darkness
I call to thee to bless me with thy bright face
Lighten my pathway through the shadows.
For I stand shrouded in the wailing dark
Awaiting the sun to rise within my soul.

Hail to thee, Hel, O Barrow's Mistress
Whose voice is heard within the echoing tomb
To where my ancestors rest within your darkness
Their knowledge and wisdom I here now seek
Awaiting your silence to still my restless mind.

Hail to thee, Hel, O Guardian of the Soul
It is your arms that reach out to draw in all who come,
Those who are lost in the endless labyrinth of despair
I find my soul in tatters and mournful at your gates
Awaiting you to clutch me to your skeleton breast.

Hail to thee, Hel, O Lady of Doom
Your word is final as you never lie
I offer you this broken vessel of my self
Overcome with burdens that leave me empty
Awaiting your bitter gift that will bring forth life.

Hail to thee, Hel, O Wisest of Wights
In the name of regeneration I call you,
My soul seeks your guidance through these dark hours
I seek you to bestow upon me your compassion
Awaiting you to grant me the fortitude from within.

Lilith by Soror Basilisk

# Commencing the Journey

In the 1992 movie *Death Becomes Her*, Goldie Horne and Meryl Streep do whatever they can to become immortal. But mortal we are and so too are the things in our life. This is one of the greatest lessons and blessings that the Dark Goddess bestows upon us. Death to all those things that hinder or hold us back, that distract and obscure us from reaching our fullest soul potential. At times such death is painful, especially if we have a lot of emotional attachment or refuse to understand its permanence.

The less open we are to change, the harder or more difficult we find our encounter with the Dark Goddess, especially when she materialises before us as Kali, cutting through the stagnation with her sword, severing unworkable ties and attachments; or as Oya, arriving on her winds of change to descend upon our lives like a category eight hurricane leaving us to pick our way through the debris that remains. The more we open ourselves up to the ebbing and flowing, the waxing and waning nature of the natural rhythms around us, the easier the result of lessons and experiences of her in our lives can be handled.

The awakening felt through the Dark Goddess need not be painful or filled with regret. It is not uncommon to feel great relief when the veil is lifted or the rose-tinted glasses are smashed, enabling the truth to be revealed. The courage is found within so we can step into and embrace fully our own authentic self through the guidance of the Dark Goddess. Just imagine the power you will be able to feel when you gain full control of your own self.

How deeply you want to work with the Dark Goddess is entirely up to you. For people who have never done any kind of soul or Shadow Work, it is recommended to first establish a connection with one of the many aspects in which she presents herself. This connection begins with creating a sacred space that will include an altar or shrine. This can be in the corner of your room, the top of a bookcase or dressing table, and the like – depending on your space and who else you share the space with. The simple act of lighting a candle often can create a sense of sacredness. The preference is yours as to whether you use scented or non-scented candles, however, if you chose to also burn incense, some scented candle may be overpowering.

Connecting with the various aspects of the Dark Goddess, or even the Dark Goddess as a concept in general, is the same as with any deity, in that this often takes four relatively simple steps:

- Know the goddess: Read the myths and if possible, learn about the culture they are from, even the era in which they were probably more widely worshipped, especially if there were any specific cultural aspects in the way in which they were worshipped.
- Build an altar that represents and honours that particular aspect of the Dark Goddess as she appears to you.
- Make offerings by lighting candles and/or incense. Some people also like to present the deity their favourite foods or alcohol, or recite prayers. The latter can be found in historical texts (such as the Orphic Hymns for Greek deities), or you may like to write something yourself that expresses what the goddess means to you.
- Meditation on establishing your connection with the particular aspect of the Dark Goddess that you wish to work with.

The construction of an altar should never be underestimated. Altars have been used throughout history as a bridge between the subconscious and the conscious realms. They are places where the scattered parts of our psyche can be reconnected through the items that are placed upon it, as well as providing a way to communicate with our higher selves. Or a spiritual sanctuary can be found throughout history, incorporating many spiritual practices and beliefs. Their construction has been so deeply etched into our human psyche that we probably have them within our homes without even realising. For example, a collection of photographs of relatives who have passed could be interpreted as an "Ancestor Shrine". Similarly, a vase of roses given to us by our beloved displayed by their photograph and selection of trinkets received could be a "Love Altar".

Your altar is a place of meditation, reflection and worship. It can be a small corner of a bookcase shelf or the top of a dressing table. Have an image or picture of the aspect of the Dark Goddess that you wish to work with. There are numerous suitable pictures available on the internet, or historical representations can be found, printed off and even laminated. You may come across a statue of your chosen aspect of the Dark Goddess, or use an item such as a seed pod (representing the chthonic nature of the Dark Goddess), or any other appropriate symbol (i.e., shell, skull, lion for Sekhmet, or a pomegranate for Persephone) as your representation. If you are artistically inclined, you may like to draw your own image.

Learn to see if there are any taboos surrounding that deity especially when it comes to making offerings, or whether there are any specific protocols that should be followed, as is the case when the comes to working with Egyptian deities. While some people may believe that such protocols is not necessary in our modern age, I am personally of the belief that if your objective is to establish a deeper connection and therefore relationship with a particular deity (which will become beneficial if you require their help at a later stage), then they should be treated as an honoured guest.

If you make a promise to the Dark Goddess, as with any deity, then make sure that you keep it. Not only do our words have power, they also have consequences. The gods are real, very real indeed. They hear our prayers, pleas and petitions. If we make a promise and do not keep our word, they may very well manifest the end desire, or their end of the bargain in some other form. Believe you me, think carefully of what you ask, i.e., if you ask for happiness in your life this may initially mean the removal of certain relationships and situations that you may initially not have even been aware were actually making you unhappy in the first place.

Remember too that you do at times need to set boundaries and remind the gods that you have bills to pay and having a job, or at least a steady form of employment, is beneficial. This is much in the same way that when, in the Greek myth, Persephone (Kore, the Maiden) was taken in to the Underworld and Demeter (her mother) went into mourning resulting in the crops not being able to grow, which in turn resulted in the Gods not receiving their offerings because the people did not have any food to eat themselves let alone make offerings to the gods. It was only then that Zeus, the chief Olympian god, stepped in and assisted Demeter, which in turn assisted the people which resulted in the crops being grown again, the people not starving and the gods again receiving their offerings.

In ancient Egyptian temples, statues of the gods were often housed in the "holy of holies" where they were kept out of sight from the general public and were bathed and dressed prior to worship commencing. The ancient Egyptians were very conscious about cleanliness so with this in mind, when connecting with Nephthys you might wish to keep her statue covered when you are not working with her, and then bathe the statue in rose water or clean fresh water prior to any work. You may also like to sprinkle "natron"[146] around your ritual space and burn handmade kyphi incense (recipe provided later in this book). Prior to working with any Egyptian deity, it is often recommended that you ensure that you are also bathed and dressed in clean clothes.

Care should be taken when selecting the types of incense you wish to burn for Egyptian deities because some incenses, particularly those from India, may contain traces of cow dung. While such incense is appropriate for Hindu deities where the cow is considered to be a sacred animal, the ancient Egyptians and therefore these gods may not look so favourably upon you if your offerings contained traces of faecal matter.

Indian supermarkets often have copper and brass offering bowls, terracotta lamps, ghee and cotton wicks, and other items that can be used when setting up an altar specifically for Hindu goddesses such as Kali and Durga.

If you do not have an altar or shrine, it is important to use your sacred space as often as you can. Simply spending a short period, say 10 to 15 minutes, every (or every other) evening lighting a candle and focusing on your intention – why are you here? What do you wish to achieve? What draws you to this work or to that particular aspect of the Dark Goddess? Meditation is often an extremely invaluable technique when it comes to spiritual and even devotional work.

Journaling is strongly recommended for all work that involves working with the Shadow Self. Are you mildly conscious about the concept of the Dark Goddess? Do you have an unresolved issue or problem that you need to reach the root cause of in order to free your soul? Have you found yourself in the sea of uncertainty or feel as if nothing "fits" anymore in your life? Are you at some kind of crossroads?

Journaling does not necessarily have to be a written essay, nor does it need to make sense. It can take the form of poetry that either you or someone else has written that you resonate with, rituals, meditations, or merely dot points that you feel personally important or reflective. It can take the form of art work, from a collage of images through which you express your feelings, experiences and emotions, to sculptures or even craft items that may assist with your journey). What is important is the outlet it provides – a way for you to express what you are going through when you journey with the Dark Goddess.

Due to the deep transformations that can occur even on the physical level, some people like to take a before and after photograph as a way of capturing this transformation. Although, it your descent into the Underworld is not voluntary, then this may be difficult to achieve.

Having a bit of an idea of why you are here can be of assistance, especially as the journey may reveal different folds and directions that may not seem all that appealing for you, especially at the initial stage. Further, having a starting point for reference is extremely beneficial to revisit weeks, months or even years down the track. Remember that such work can be life changing and what we "receive" may not be what we (our ego) actually contemplated – for we are often working at a much deeper soul level and with the subconscious.

# Gifts from the Dark Goddess

The underlying theme for many Dark Goddesses mentioned in this book is transformation through some kind of "death". The word "death" tends to be feared in our Western culture despite it being a natural process. This could be because not only does it remind us of our mortality, but it is often something that we feel we do not have control over. Yet, within Buddhist teachings, it is death that has the certainty while life is the uncertainty. Any persistence we may have to be in control of things that are actually beyond our abilities can prevent us from adapting to changing situations. Despite what we may tell ourselves, life is unpredictable and when our soul needs change at a deeper level, we will often find ourselves in situations where such change appears to be forced upon us, i.e., facing serious health issues.

Being forced to step into the unknown, or even learning to let go and surrender to forces beyond our control (whether it is some form of deity or the universe) is uncomfortable and at times even frightening. The end result, however, is transformation, not only of our own selves but also our soul on a deeper level.

The Dark Goddess shatters the old, outdated, outworn structures in our lives and forces us (if we are not willing to accept) to embrace change and the new. She does away with our rose-tinted glasses that we comfortably see the world through, tests our courage, resolve and even beliefs, all with the purpose of enabling us to be reborn with a new awakening state of awareness, consciousness, and even curiosity about the world in which we reside, especially the deeper mysteries that lie hidden in the shadow (subconscious) realms. The truth is that we cannot progress spiritually unless we are willing to sacrifice (give) something – and that something is often our "smaller" selves, our attachment to everyday pleasures and comforts that, in the great scheme of things, are often short lived as they are things attached to our lower ego self, not our higher spiritual self. This "sacrifice" need not mean you should become a hermit and denounce all the trappings of modern life. Our willingness to let go of attachments is a form of sacrifice that only we can make, for what we are doing is not necessarily "giving up" something. Instead, it means to become more consciously aware that all living things are interconnected. After all the word "sacrifice" comes from the Latin *sacer* meaning "sacred rite". Maybe you can draw inspiration from the writings of 17th century poet and mystic Thomas Traherne who wrote:

> "You'll never enjoy the world aright till the sea itself floweth in your veins
> And you are clothed with the heavens and crowned with the stars."[147]

The other gift that the Dark Goddess teaches is the wisdom of letting go of attachments, and opening our eyes to the "needs" as opposed to the "wants" that are place upon us to distract us from seeking the deeper truths. In doing this she pushes us to move beyond our insular self of ego and physiology, and to consider the greater concept, that we are merely energy that ebbs and flows, that waxes and wanes.

The Dark Goddess forces us to consider our motives, our emotional contracts and connections with other people in our lives, and most importantly, to take ownership and responsibility of our own "stuff", all the while lessening our involvement with the "stuff" that belongs to other people. We need to reassess what we deem important to spend our time and energy on.

She exposes the dirty little secrets that we keep ignoring, our feelings of resentment, anger, jealousy, and loathing towards ourselves as well as towards others. She forces us to address these feelings instead of continually sweeping them under the carpet. She brings and exposes things we ignore, deny and refuse to accept about ourselves. All our skeletons are rattled as she not only opens the closet but empties it right before our eyes. For it is only when this brutal action occurs that we find ourselves truly free and liberated.

The Dark Goddess breaks in order to make. She teaches us that to truly appreciate the light, we first must descend into the darkness. It is the ability to balance both the dark and the light within our own selves that will assist us when we navigate our way through the abyss and emerge transformed, initiated into the mysteries that the Dark Goddess rules over.

"So long as you haven't experienced this: to die and so to grow
You are only a troubled guest on the dark earth."[148]

In one version of a Dark Goddess ritual that I led, participants were instructed to write down up to seven precious things in their lives. Unbeknown to them the list was to be burnt at a later stage. Most participants were able to do this task without much hesitation save for an expression of sadness or emptiness. After the ritual had concluded a few shared that this action made them begin to reassess what they had previously felt important in their lives. It is so easy to get caught up in the superficial surface 'stuff", things that relate more to our outer world personality and the image that we project out into the world, as opposed to focusing on the deeper aspects of our lives that are only found at the deep soul level.

The Morrigan by Soror Basilisk

# Dark Goddess Workings

## Connecting with the Dark Goddess

Many people assume that you can only connected with the Dark Goddess during the waning or dark phase of the moon, or that her associated colour is black. As far as I am aware this assumption, as pointed out in Part I, tends to stem from the connection between the goddess and the moon first made by Jane Ellen Harrison[149] and later by Robert Graves[150], where the Dark Goddess equated to the Crone aspect of the Triple Goddess, and therefore was connected with the dark phase of the moon. As we have seen, many goddesses that fall under the category of being "dark" do not fit the Crone aspect. Therefore, you can certainly connect with the Dark Goddess at any time regardless of what phase the moon is in.

Like any other aspect of the goddess, the Dark Goddess is there whenever you need her, and there are times when she will make her presence known without invitation. The only difference is that unless you have built up a specific relationship with her, or are familiar with her ways, you may not always be aware of her guidance. As to colour, goddesses such as the Morrigan, Kali and Hekate all have red as their chosen colour. Oya likes burgundy or aubergine purple colours. When I work with Ereshkigal, she tends to favour a midnight or dark blue colours. You may find yourself drawn to use these colours or even different ones when you work with them.

The following ritual is designed to help you establish your connection with the Dark Goddess. The preferred phase of the moon to perform this ritual is during the waning or dark phase, because on a subconscious energetic level our energies are naturally moving inward. If you are not familiar with when this occurs, I would recommend that you purchase a Moon Diary (there are a number about) or visit internet sites such as timeanddate.com where you enter where you live to get the exact time of whatever phase of the moon that you are after.

Other objects you will require for this ritual include a candle (it can be of any colour that resonates to you, preference is a darker colour), incense, anointing oil[151] and a black crystal of your choice. For example, you can use jet, onyx, obsidian, black tourmaline or hematite.

Cast your circle in a manner that you are familiar with, moving in a widdershins direction (clockwise in the Southern Hemisphere and anticlockwise in the Northern Hemisphere). You might like to burn some incense that has Underworld qualities such as patchouli, myrrh, frankincense, styrax or juniper.

Call upon the goddess in her dark aspect in whatever words that resonate to you. You may, however, like to use the following invocation:

*Maiden of the Shadows, Mother of Darkness,*
*Queen of the Underworld,*
*I beseech you.*
*Enter this sacred place I have created for you.*
*Bestow upon me the vision to see into the dark.*
*Guide me into the Mysteries that you rule over.*
*Granting me the wisdom of my own abyss.*
*Be here now.*

Anoint your candle by applying a small amount of oil near the wick of the candle and moving down to the base. As you do this, focus on visualising yourself being open and receiving any insights the Dark Goddess has to offer. Ensure that you keep open and clear to what may occur as messages can often come in the form of symbols. This is a great time to use any divination technique, such as mirror scrying or tarot, or guided meditation.

Refresh your incense as an offering to the Dark Goddess. If you have a desire to hum or chant, or even to remain quiet, do whatever feels appropriate to you.

Hold your crystal and draw the energy of the Dark Goddess into it, visualising the candle flame as the source of wisdom in the dark.

After you have connected with the Dark Goddess, thank her for her wise counsel and for revealing her Mysteries to you. It is often considered appropriate to leave an offering for the Dark Goddess. This can be in the form of an apple, pomegranate or wine. Some goddesses have specific offerings associated with them. If you are indoors, you can take your offering outside after you have finished your ritual to leave. Offerings to Hekate, for example, are traditionally left at a crossroads.

Close your circle in your usual manner and ground any excess energy. Carry your crystal with you (maybe in a small pouch) to receive any continuing insights and knowledge that the Dark Goddess will bestow upon you.

## Ways of Exploring Your Shadow Self

Art Therapy: Regardless of whether you have an artistic side or not, explore your shadow self through creating something. This could include scribbling random words or doodling on a page. Allow yourself to simply put pen to paper and see what it creates as you explore your deeper thoughts, fears, desires and archetypal selves.

Meditate on your first four chakras: Muladhara (root, at the base of the spine), svadhisthana (sacral, below the navel), manipura (solar plexus, above the navel) and anahata (heart).

Open Monitoring Meditation: Take on the role of observer and be open for any and all emotions, thoughts and ideas to come into your consciousness. Explore, without any judgement, your "light" (positive) and "dark" (negative) aspects. Take note of what comes to the surface and accept these feelings and emotions unconditionally, without any judgement.

Keep a "Shadow" work book: Record when these aspects

appear and then explore them by asking "why?" For example, when you come across a shadow trait or thought, ask yourself "but why?" When you get to that answer, ask "but why?" again. This self-questioning can help to get to the root cause, the underlying issue of a situation.

Note: Keep in mind that this work should never be used in place of counselling or other forms of therapy when it comes to dealing with deep rooted issues. In such circumstances, it is always strongly recommended that you seek professional help.

## Making a Shadow Mask

Masks have been used for thousands of years to honour the many faces of spirit. They have also been used as a way to connect and deepen personal relationships with deity. When we create a Shadow Mask, we call upon that aspect of ourselves that may be hidden or ignored in the darkness, and bring it forth into the light. This provides us with a deep form of healing, celebration and even freedom.

Begin with a stack of eight to ten pieces of alfoil (aluminium foil), each piece large enough to cover your face. Once stacked, scrunch the pieces together and then straighten them back out as this will help them staying together. Place the alfoil stack over your face, moulding to your features, especially over your nose, mouth and eye sockets. Ensure that you also mould the alfoil stack against the sides of your face. The alfoil mask should cover your entire face, from hairline to chin, or for a half mask, it should cover from forehead to nose.

Cut out the eye holes and trim the excess foil from the edges of the mask as well. Cut small slits into any curved areas, overlap the slits and then tape them together to keep the curve shape. Cut a 2.5cm slit into each side of the forehead, overlap the slits to create a curved edge, then then tape them together with masking tape. Repeat this for the chin if this is a full-face mask. The more you overlap the slits, the deeper the curve will be. Reinforce other cut edges including the eyes with masking tape.

Cover the mask with at least three layers of papier mâché. Do this by mixing together equal parts of glue (or flour) and water, then tear newspaper into thin strips about 2.5 cm wide and up to 10cm long), and dip the strips into the paste, before smoothing them over the mask. Use smaller strips around the eyes and nose. Apply the first two layers right on top of each other, and let them dry for up to an hour before applying the third layer. Let the mask dry completely.

Ensure that you fold the newspaper strips over the cut edges of the mask, including the eye holes. This will prevent the alfoil from scratching you. For a nicer finish you can cover the inside of the mask with one layer of papier mâché as well. Once dry, you can decorate it however you wish so that it represents your Shadow Self. Some people just paint their masks, others decorate them with feathers, ribbons, stickers, pieces of material, and other craft pieces. You are only limited by your imagination.

If you are not able to make your mask from scratch, craft shops and even newsagents may stock papier mâché masks that you can then decorate yourself.

## Making, Cleansing and Using a Scrying Mirror

Find an old wooden or metal picture frame, preferably dark in colour and no larger than 30cm diameter. Remove and thoroughly clean the glass using a few drops of vinegar mixed in some water. Once dry, paint one side of the glass with black high gloss enamel paint that is suitable for glass. To ensure a flawless effect, it is best to apply two coats, ensuring the first coat is dry before applying the second coat.

When the paint is completely dry, place the glass back into the finished frame with the unpainted side facing outwards, and your scrying mirror is complete.

Before using, however, it is recommended that your scrying mirror should be cleansed. The following herbal infusion wash is ideal because it does not contain harsh chemicals that can be found in many household glass cleaning products. Instead the metaphysical attributes of the specific herbs listed help to purify the energy of your scrying mirror while also clearing away dust, dirt and other human-imposed imperfections from its surface.

Word of Caution: If you are pregnant, pennyroyal essential oil should be omitted due to there being evidence that this essential oil can cause abortions by causing the uterus to contract.[152] If in doubt, please check with your doctor or health professional.

Bring two standard tablespoons each of mugwort and chamomile into two cups of water to a slow rolling boil in a medium saucepan. Reduce the heat, and simmer the mixture for ten minutes. Then add six drops of pennyroyal essential oil (** omit if you are pregnant as advised above).

Simmer the mixture on low heat for a further three minutes, and then allow the mixture to cool to room temperature. Strain the liquid through a piece of cheesecloth into a bowl.

Soak a cotton ball in the herbal infused mixture, and rub over the surface of the mirror. Rinse the mirror with fresh water before allowing the mirror to air-dry.

You do not need to cleanse your mirror using the above method prior to using it, only whenever it looks or even when it feels like it needs a cleanse. When not being used, it is recommended to keep your scrying mirror covered with a black silk or cotton cloth, or stored in a bag.

To use your scrying mirror, in a darkened room, position one or two candles where they will not interfere with your line of vision, and sit or stand comfortably directly in front of the mirror. Stare into the mirror. Do not worry about blinking because it is perfectly fine if you do.

Take note of any patterns, symbols or pictures that may form, as well as any thoughts that may appear in your head that seem to have nothing at all to do with anything. The length of time you scry is entirely up to you. It may be for a few moments, or it may be longer, even up to an hour. You should stop when you begin to feel restless, or if you are becoming distracted by mundane things.

It is recommended that you record what your experiences are in your diary or journal as messages often come to us in many subtle forms that we may not necessarily initially recognise. When we record our experiences, this enables us to reflect at a later date, allowing our unconscious mind time to process things. It is also possible that we may receive messages for other people within our circle of family and friends.

## Dark Moon Ritual

The dark phase of the moon is a luminal time when the moon exhibits no illumination at all in the night sky. When the first sliver of light begins to appear, then technically this is the time of the new moon. Online calendars such as "Moon Giant"[153] provide illumination percentages which will enable you to plan the more auspicious times for undertaking specific dark moon rituals.

Before you undertake this ritual make a list of personality traits that you feel are holding you back from achieving your desires and goals, or even spiritual advancement. These may be emotional attachments, jealousy, anger, negative thought patterns, and the like.

To begin the ritual, ground and centre yourself using your preferred manner. If you are new to ritual work, then as you inhale imagine that you are breathing in a golden energy that circulates throughout your body. As you exhale, imagine that you are breathing out a murky coloured energy that represents stress, tension, things no longer wanted or needed in your life. When you feel grounded and centred within yourself, look at the list you have constructed to see what is holding you back from spiritual advancement. You may wish to meditate on these things for a short period of time so that they are clearly focused in your mind.

When you are ready, look into your scrying mirror and see yourself as you currently are, as you will be, and as you have been. As you look at your reflection ask: What ails thee?" Wait and hear what the image tells you. Ensure that you write all the things that come to you down in your diary or journal as these are a part of the issues that hold you back. Choose one of these issues to work on through to the full moon of the current cycle.

Once you have determined what issue you wish to address or remove from your life, create a project that represents it. This project can be as simple or elaborate as you want, and can take the form of a drawn or painted image, a craft piece or simply as words written on a piece of paper. Attempt to work on your project daily in order to infuse it with your intention and energy. This is because the more energy you put into the project, the more effective it will be. When you are not working on your project, wrap it in a piece of silk or cotton in order to contain its energy.

At the full moon, kindle a special sacred fire and burn your project. As your project burns your desire will travel on the astral plane, sending a beacon to the universe of the energies you wish to remove from your life or bring into it. This process, while it may seem strange, has been used in temples for many hundreds, if not thousands, of years. Petitions (prayers), candles and incense, and some food items, have long been burnt on sacred fires to the gods (or the universe) in order for desires to be addressed. It is believed that once such offering is made, the gods (or the universe) will begin to send lessons and opportunities your way that will enable you to achieve your desires. You may find an immediate energy shift that night or in the coming days. Sometimes it will occur with more subtle changes.

## Spell for Breaking the Habit of Negative Thinking
The dark moon is a time for ridding oneself of bad habits,

banishing and binding spells, understanding oneself and also for spells that require justice to be brought to bear. It is also an auspicious time to work magic against attackers, as well as for understanding your own anger and passion.

For this spell you will need:

- A black "intent" candle
- A piece of black material, preferably cotton that is at least 10cm square
- Black ribbon or cord that is at least 20cm long
- A symbol that represents your habit drawn on a piece of parchment paper.
- A pinch of the following easily obtainable herbs into a small bowl: black pepper, ginger, chili powder, juniper berries, and clove
- A small black crystal (such as black onyx) or even a black river stone

Ground and centre in your usual manner. When you feel ready state aloud the following intent:

*To banish a bad habit,*
*I come before the Dark Goddess in this hour,*
*To banish negative thinking,*
*I call upon the Dark Goddess for the power!*

Light the black "intent" candle. Spread the piece of black material out before you and in the centre of it place the parchment paper upon which you have drawn a symbol that represents the habit you want to remove. Say the following:

*Bad habit of negative thinking,*
*No longer sweet, to me you are sour,*
*I confine you to this pouch,*

*Over me you have no power!*

On top of the parchment empty the bowl of herbs. As you do, repeat the above chant a second time.

Finally, on top of the herbs, place your small crystal or river rock. As you do, repeat the above chant for a third and final time.

Carefully gather together each of the four corners of the piece of material so that the contents are in the centre. Give the material a couple of twists and then wrap the ribbon or cord around and knot tightly, securing the contents inside the pouch. Say the following:

*With this knot I seal this spell*
*With the power of three times three*
*Now this charm will do its work*
*Blessed be, so mote it be!*

Open your circle in your usual manner. Place candle somewhere safe where it can burn out such as on the kitchen sink. Then bury the spell pouch somewhere that you rarely go and where it will not be dug up by animals or discovered by another person.

## Crafting a Binding Poppet

Note: Before you bind someone, it is important to understand that there is a belief that you actually bind an aspect of yourself to that particular person. For this reason, I am careful when it comes to binding people. My preference is to "encourage" the person to move out of my life by severing connections (including emotional and energetic attachments). This may come in the form of them acquiring a promotion at work or entering into a relationship that will see them leave my area. Alternatively, I ensure that my energetic boundaries and protection shields are firm.

A poppet is usually a cloth doll[154] that uses "sympathetic magic" or the Law of Attraction, incorporating the concept of like attracting like. You can create a poppet to represent a particular person (even yourself) in that it is believed that anything that happens to the poppet will affect the person it represents. As such, poppets can be constructed to attract (or keep) a lover, to heal a person (including yourself), to protect, or even banish a person from your life.

For a basic poppet construction, cut some fabric (my personal preference is to use natural fibre such as cotton or calico) into a shape that resembles a human shape – i.e., a head, with arms and legs extending from the body, although this is not essential. You will need a front and a back which you will hand sew together using either a running or blanket stitch securely, leaving the top of the head open. The poppet is then filled with a combination of appropriate herbs associated with your preferred purpose of the poppet, batting or filler (to bulk out the doll), and any personal items that will link the poppet to a person (if needed).

Once you have prepared your poppet, if it is to represent a person, you then "tie" it to that person by naming it. If the poppet is for a general reason, i.e., protection of your house, then this does not need to be done. It is your choice as to how detailed you make your poppet, depending on the situation.

If the poppet is to represent a specific person then use the following charm or something similar:

*This little person that I have made*
*I give you life, I give you a name* [name of the person]
*Her/his/their\* body is your body*
*Her/his/their breath is your breath*
*Her/his/their passion is your passion*
*Her/his/their blood is your blood*
*Be like this person, for you are now one*
*The link of unison has begun.*

\* Use only the word which is appropriate.

If you have someone in your life who is causing you a great deal of stress then you may wish to make a poppet that will banish them completely from your life. For this, use black material to make your poppet shape and then fill it with sawdust or dried herbs. If you have any hair or nail clippings from the person, add that as well. Once you have completed making the poppet, light a candle, hold the poppet up and say:

*This doll represents* [name of the person]
*I wish* [name of the person] *no harm,*
*I am performing now a binding charm.*
*I will bind them well with ropes of love,*
*Lest I anger those above.*
*I will remember now the rule of three,*
*What I give out returns to me*

Wrap some black ribbon around the part of the poppet that is causing the harm, e.g., the mouth of a liar or the arms if the person is being violent. As you wrap, say:

*This ribbon binds you tight,*
*Against its magic you cannot fight.*
*You will cease to do others harm,*
*After I finish this magic charm.*
*I bind you* [name of the person]
*I bind you* [name of the person]
*I bind you* [name of the person].

Repeat chanting the last line until you have finished wrapping the ribbon around the poppet. Imagine the person being completely wrapped and being prevented from causing harm. Place the poppet on a shelf where it will be safe. Every time you pass it, say:

*This ribbon that bound you tight,*
*Against its magic you could not fight.*
*You will cease to do others harm,*
*Now I have finished this magic charm.*

When you feel that the person has stopped harming others, unbind the ribbon, and say:

*This poppet has served me well,*
*It no longer represents* [name of the person].

Take the poppet apart and bury all the pieces in the ground.

## Diminishing Another's Power

The following may be of benefit if you find yourself in a situation where another person appears to have a rather manipulating influence over you, despite you strengthening your boundaries.

You will need:

- About 60cm length of natural twine or string
- A bowl of cold water
- A pair of scissors or a small knife to cut the string
- A container to put the string in.

After creating your sacred space, gather all your ingredients together. Hold the ends of the string so that it creates a loop. Hold the loop end so that the individual ends hang into the bowl of water. This means that when you pull the string towards you, the end of the string will move through the water, thus cleansing the string.

Visualise the connection between you and the other person. As you do this, visualise the string beginning to glow with the negative energy they are sending you. Your hands are the wire that this energy travels along. Begin to pull the string slowly towards you. As you do this, visualise that you are pulling their energy towards you.

Say the following:

*When you push, I shall pull.*
*When you strike, I move away*
*Drawing you deeper into my grasp*
*Your power is mine to move as my own*
*Water cleanses it.*
*Now it is mine.*

As the cord moves through the water really visualise it being cleansed, the water washing away the negative intent and leaving the cord as a crackling live wire of magical energy.

See the energy pulled from the source into the loop and when the time is right, cut the cord and say:

*Now I free myself.*

The cord can be used to effect whatever magic you want, or it can be burned. My personal preference is to burn the cord so that your connection with the person is completely destroyed as is their hold over you.

## Banishing Spell

When performing banishing spells, the result may work in unexpected ways. For example, the person may suddenly decide to move away, or get another job. They may have a change of heart and turn into a decent person, or go through a streak of bad luck where they have to learn their lessons the hard way. There is always the possibility that if they are projecting enough negative energy, they may very well end up hurt. Remember of the Law of Attraction mentioned earlier – like attracts like.

For the following Banishing Spell, you will need to make a

Banishing Oil from essential oils. Be careful with these oils as they are skin irritants. If you are sensitive to essential oils, then you may wish to stick with the olive oil on its own.

To make the Banishing Oil, add 15 drops of pine essential oil, 12 drops of rue essential oil, seven drops of pepper essential oil, and 10 drops of peppermint essential oil into 15mls of olive oil (or any other carrier oil you prefer to use).

Make a poppet out of black cloth, stuff it with cotton balls or batting, adding any hair or nail clippings of the person if you have any. Sew the poppet close and stitch a picture of the person to the front of the poppet (if you have one). Into a black candle, carve the person's name and add the runes Thurisaz (resembles a "P" Þ), Isa (resembles an "I" |), and Eihwaz (resembles a pointed "S" ᛇ). Also carve into the candle the symbol for the dark moon (a filled in circle), widdershins[155] (a clockwise spiral with an arrowhead at the end), and Bars (tic-tac-toe with four vertical lines and four crossing horizontal lines).

Anoint the poppet and candle with Banishing Oil made above. (If you are not able to make the Banishing Oil, then a single essential oil with banishing properties can be used.)

Prepare your sacred space in your usual manner. Light the carved candle and hold the poppet out in front of you. Say:

*Creature of cloth thou art,*
*Now creature of flesh and blood you be.*
*I name you* [name of the person you are binding].
*No more shall you do me harm,*
*No more shall you spread false tales,*
*No more shall you interfere in my life, nor in the lives of my loved*
 *ones.*
*By the power of the gods and by my will,*
*So mote it be!*

Take a long length of red ribbon and begin to wrap the poppet like a mummy, taking care that you do not leave any space unwrapped. As you wrap the ribbon, say:

*I bind your feet from bringing you to harm me.*
*I bind your hands from reaching out to harm me.*
*I bind your mouth from spreading rumours to harm me.*
*I bind your mind from sending energy to harm me.*
*If you continue, may all negative energy return directly to you.*

Tie off the ribbon tightly. Hold the poppet and imagine all negative energy that this person has sent to you being reflected back to them. Wrap the poppet in black cloth and tie with another length of ribbon, and say:

*Dark Goddess, I have bound this person*
*From harming me and my loved ones.*
*By the powers of three times three*
*By earth and fire, air and sea*
*I fix this spell, then set it free*
*'Twill give no harm to return on me*
*As I will, so mote it be!*

Allow the candle burn out in a safe place while the poppet sits at its base. Then take the poppet and the remains of the candle far from your home and bury it deep in the ground so that it will not be dug up any time soon.

## An Assortment of Incense Recipes

The following incense recipes have come from various sources and are to be burnt over charcoal disks. If you prefer to use joss sticks or cones, then if the Dark Goddess you are working with does not have a specific incense, then Night Queen (or any other jasmine base), myrrh or even frankincense are often appropriate.

- **Altar:** 1 part frankincense, ½ part myrrh and ¼ part cinnamon.
- **Baba Yaga:** Equal parts of dried sunflower petals, bay leaves, and copal.
- **Banishing:** 1 part each of bay leaves, cinnamon, red wine, rose petals, myrrh, and sea salt. Burn when performing banishing spells to remove unwanted energies, or spirits from the home.
- **Cleansing:** ½ part each of wood betony, burdock and white sage, and ½ part each of clove, lavender, rosemary, thyme and wormwood.
- **Divination:** 2 parts sandalwood, 1 part orange peel, ½ part each of mace and cinnamon.
- **Dark Goddess:** 1 part each patchouli, red sandalwood and benzoin sumatra.
- **Dark Moon #1:** 1 part each of dried jasmine flowers, rose petals and myrrh resin, ½ part dried elder flowers. Add a few drops of myrrh essential oil.
- **Dark Moon #2:** 2 parts each of copal and sandalwood, 1 part dried rose petals, a few drops of myrrh essential oil.
- **Dream:** 2 parts Sandalwood, 1 part each of rose and camphor, and a few drops of jasmine essential oil.
- **Egyptian Kyphi:** 1 part each of frankincense, storax, Balm of Gilead buds (ground) and cassia or cinnamon, a few drops each of lotus and musk oil. The ancient Egyptians also added honey and wine to the mixture which you can do if you like. Add only a little and let the incense dry prior to use. Use for banishing and purification.
- **Ereshkigal:** Equal parts of blessed thistle, bay laurel and rosemary.
- **Five Resin Protection:** 2 parts frankincense, 1 part each of copal and myrrh, ½ part each of dragon's blood and gum arabic.
- **Hekate #1:** 3 parts sandalwood, 2 parts cypress, 1 part

spearmint.

- **Hekate #2**: 1 part each of dried bay leaves, dried mint, and thyme, a pinch each of myrrh and frankincense, 13 drops cypress essential oil, and 3 drops camphor oil. Combine and store in a tightly-capped jar for at least two weeks before using.
- **Hel**: 2 parts fir pine needles, 1 part each juniper berries and thyme, ½ part crushed wild garlic, and 1 bundle Mountain Queen wildflower (*Saxifraga cotyledon*).
- **Kali**: 1 part each of sandalwood chips and dried jasmine flowers, ½ part dried rose petals, and two drops of your own blood (menstrual blood preferred).
- **Kyphi** (traditional): ¾ part honey, 3 raisins, ¼ part each copal, myrrh, orris and storax, 1 part sandalwood, ½ part each frankincense and cinnamon bark, red wine (to moisten mixture), and benzoin (to roll balls in). Thoroughly grind all ingredients separately, then mix together red wine to moisten. Shape into small balls and roll in benzoin. Dry for at least a week until firm.
- **Lilith**: Equal parts of peony, rose petals, mugwort, sandalwood, white sage, and patchouli.
- **Medusa**: Equal parts of frankincense, myrrh and storax.
- **Morgan le Fay**: 1 part each of dragon's blood and wormwood, and a pinch black pepper.
- **Nephthys**: 4 parts frankincense, 3 parts Gum Arabic, 2 parts myrrh, 1 part each cedar, juniper, calamus and cinnamon. This incense can be used for any Egyptian deity.
- **Persephone**: Equal parts of frankincense and storax. I sometimes add some pomegranate juice.
- **Purification**: 2 parts each of sandalwood and bay, 1 part each of cinnamon and vervain, a pinch of salt. Burn with windows open to clear a room with disturbed energy.
- **Overcome Opposition**: ¾ part cloves, ½ part each of garlic, sweet woodruff and red clover, and ¼ part High

John the Conqueror.

- **Sekhmet:** Equal parts of frankincense, copal and myrrh.
- **The Morrigan**: 1 part rosemary, ½ part each of patchouli and myrrh, and 7 drops musk oil.
- **Tiamat**: 3 parts cedar, 2 parts juniper, 1 part each cypress and tamarisk. This incense can be used for any Babylonia deity.

**Please note that you should not burn any incense when working with Oya as she does not like smoke.

## Herbal Dream Pillow

The following herbs selected for making dream pillows are for stimulating the intuitive and psychic centres, and are meant to prevent nightmares and promote restful sleep. They are to help you drift off to sleep naturally. You can use any material that you like, however, muslin or cotton is preferred.

Begin by cutting two identical sizes of fabric that are appropriately 12cm square (although any size will do). With the wrong sides of the material together, stitch three sides to the depth of 2cm. In the fourth side, leave a gap about 3cm wide. Turn the bag right side out so that the seams are on the inside.

Begin filling your bag with your own herbal mixture or use the following blend that consists of 1 part each of lavender flowers (peace of mind), rose petals (clairvoyance), chamomile (to induce a restful sleep), bay leaves (dreams, visions and protection), calendula (clairvoyant dreams and protection while sleeping), and vervain (freedom from nightmares).

Be careful not to overfill your dream pillow as it should go unnoticed when slipped inside the pillow case.

Once the bag is filled to your liking, complete the herbal pillow by stitching the gap on the fourth side by hand.

Sekhmet by Soror Basilisk

# Call to Hekate

(By Frances Billinghurst, 2015)

Come, O Lady of Mysteries,
Come unto me
The silvery silence of the moon
Reveals thy innermost pathway.
Grant me access to thy sacred realm.

Come, O Threefold Mistress,
Come unto me
I await thy presence at the crossroads
Travelling between the realms I come
To seek for thee.

Come, O Keeper of the Keys
Come unto me
Permit me entry into thy innermost chamber
Where my soul lies bare for thee
Awaiting your illumination.

Night prowler, ancient one, come unto me
Shape-shifter, transformer, I beseech thee
Look favourably upon my offering
My sacrifice I offer up to thee
Come, O Hekate, come
Come unto me.

# My Personal Encounters with the Dark Goddess

Anyone who works with the Dark Goddess has their own story and what follows is mine in all its rawness. While I have already disclosed part of my more recent encounter with the Dark Goddess, in this section I will start from the beginning.

I cannot remember when I first journeyed into her realm, for it appears to be a place I would often find myself, not through trauma or repression, at least not initially, but I seemed to have a natural affinity with her and the Underworld realms.

Maybe this attraction was natural for someone who often felt they were living on the fringe, subconsciously deemed not completely worthy enough, or indeed interested in, the increasing superficialness of the world around them. From early adolescence, the transfer from primary school to high school may have had something to do with this dissociation with the Upper World. Yet I cannot honesty recall a specific incident. All I remember is that I would often find myself on the outer rim, the outside of the circle of popularity due to increasing bouts of self-consciousness that were subsequently perceived as shyness (or aloofness). This later emerged into the realisation that I was actually introverted in character. This saw me draw more and more to the boundaries where the temptation of being swallowed up or hidden by the encroaching shadows rendered much relief. Over time it was within this shadowy half-light world where I sought comfort. Yet being an introvert, this desire to be by myself fought with a longing to be included, to run with the popular circle. Ebbing and flowing, the need to be included yet the desire to be by myself continued to plague me until I read Susan Cain's *Quiet: The Power of Introverts in a World That Can't Stop Talking*[156], and realised that it was perfectly okay to prefer my own company.

Having discovered the concept of the goddess, the diving feminine, in the late 1990s, I would often work with a chosen aspect of the Dark Goddess through meditating on her attributed myth. In one instance in particular I was crafting a magical rite with four particular aspects that we had called upon, each associated with a particular element, when Hekate barged in, demanding to know why she was not included with the other goddesses who we had invoked in the ritual. I was surprised, both with her appearance and her abruptness. As it was, my fellow ritualists and I had not included her because two days earlier we had performed a rite especially for her and her alone. When asked by other people just how I actually knew that it was Hekate, the best answer I can give is that I just "knew". She did not appear physically but I received an image, a vision, similar to that of a dream while we were meditating. The more interesting point is that a fellow ritualist also received a similar vision.

The next major encounter occurred in 2008 while I was attending a goddess conference where I found myself on the banks of a river crying uncontrollably. Even as the tears rolled down my face, I could feel an aspect of my being had detached itself and was watching me. This in itself was an unusual experience to go through. I cannot recall what set me off on this spiral of what turned out to be rather self-indulgent grief and loss, but suddenly appearing in my vision was she, in the guise of a leather clad warrior from the deck of tarot cards that I had been working with at the time. Her message was simple: "Wear your crown. Act as you have been instructed to do."

It was a number of years later when I truly experience the awesomeness of the Dark Goddess which was completely different and more profound to that which I had experienced up to this point. Instead of sneaking through the backdoor, so to speak, I found myself at the first gate to Ereshkigal's Underworld when in July 2015 I was diagnosed with Stage 2 (early) breast cancer. Whether it was primarily the early detection or that coupled with my 20 plus years' interest in metaphysics, I found the overall experience strangely empowering and liberating, yet far reaching as it completely turned my world upside down.

In an extremely short period of time the veil behind which a number of people who classified themselves as "friends" was lifted, exposing the gut-wrenching truth that such "friendships" were sadly often one sided, i.e., when they needed something from me I would hear from them, however, now when the need was on the other foot, their life was far more important. As my attention and energy turned inwards to myself, I subconsciously released not only them from any obligation they initially made when I was first diagnosed, but myself from any self-imposed expectation that, as I had been there for them in the past, they would automatically be there for me during my "hour of need". This releasing would eventually allow new relationships to be established.

As the months continued, I realised that my coping mechanism of operating in survival mode was having a detrimental effect as it gave the outward impression that I was "coping". Maybe I was. On another level, however, it felt very different. The abruptness of my life change could be likened to Persephone's Maiden aspect of Kore, however, when the ground opened up, instead of Hades rising up and snatching me from the Upper World, I fell. I then became like Inanna as the long winding process took me deeper and deeper through the levels of my inner self as aspects of my life were stripped away from me, physically, emotionally, psychologically and even spiritually. Change was occurring at all levels of my being. It was constant and unrelenting. Any illusion, belief or conditioning of my pre-diagnosed existence felt as if it was being brought before a judge (my deep soul self) and questioned.

I found a safe place deep in the Underworld where I could be off the radar and therefore able to protect myself as I struggled to deal with being so exposed and vulnerable. I was learning to release, to be flexible, to not hold on to things while watching more and more aspects of the life I once knew continue to slip through my fingers like grains of sand. The deeper in the Underworld I went, the more comfortable I felt.

My treatment for breast cancer ended in November 2016, some 18 months following my initial diagnosis. Around the same time, it was made public that Olivia Newton John had been diagnosed with metastatic (advanced or secondary) breast cancer, some 25 years after her initial diagnosis when she was 44 years, only a few years younger than myself. According to my medical team, my "illness was "cured" and I was deemed "fit for work". There was no mention of the possibility of my cancer metastasising, so like Inanna, it appeared to be time for me to ascend from the Underworld. Little did I realise that the masks I had created as a coping mechanism appeared to have fooled everyone, including myself. Likewise, the effect of having lost all sense of self-identity to the extent that I did not know the person in the mirror who looked back at me, would have on a deeper psychological sense, especially when the grains of my previous life continued to slip through my fingers.

A month after my treatment finished, my then partner of nearly 11 years decided to end our relationship. The reasoning given was because I had "changed" and they had felt "neglected". Seven months later my best friend, who had been going through her own cancer journey, caught pneumonia and died. Then my mother was diagnosed. Each time I felt that I made headway in clawing my way out of the Underworld, I lost my grip and began to slip downwards again, tumbling like Alice down the rabbit hole. However, even then Alice's action was at least part voluntary as she decided to follow the rabbit. I was caught up in some endless churning ocean rip where one minute I felt in control of my life, then the next I was being dragged somewhere without any knowledge of where I was heading. I then made a spontaneous decision to undertake a spiritual retreat in Bali.

Cancer had left me detached spiritually, and having been a spiritual person for most of my life, I found this rather disturbing. Prior to this trip in 2017 I had no interest in visiting this holiday island until the opportunity presented itself for me to work with an Australian born, then Bali resident, Hindu trained high priestess. During the week we visited various sites sacred to the Balinese and underwent a series of deeply immersive spiritual practices. In one particular cave temple I experienced a number of visions as well as physical convulsions, then felt as if part of me had regressed back to a time that pre-dated any history I was aware of. There was an attempt to speak what appeared to be a forgotten ancient language yet my vocal cords simply could not formulate. During a meditation at another site I experienced the strong desire to rise out of my physical body as it felt possessed.

When I returned to Australia, I felt as if I were caught in a washing machine stuck on the constant spin cycle. My soul felt caged and I simply did not want to be interacting in all "normality". When I contacted the priestess I had travelled with, all she told me was to "meditate". At first, I rebelled against this suggestion, but eventually I surrendered to this. After all, when you find yourself standing at the precipice where you cannot see the bottom, the only option is to jump, and "trust" the process. "Trust" was something I struggled with as I had "trusted" that other people would have been there for me during my treatment only to find that they were not. This time, however, I was not disappointed. My surrendering to the meditation process enabled me to find a place of inner peace and calmness amongst the turmoil that was happening in my life.

I returned to Bali some four months later in search of a part of my soul I felt I had left behind, only to experience more revelations and personal experiences including aspecting, or channelling. My logical self had no idea of how to cope with this spiritual "invasion". Again all that seemed left for me was to surrender to the process through meditation and reciting mantras, as I realised that while my physical journey with cancer may have ended (although part of me wonders whether it will return as it did with Olivia Newton John, despite what my medical team has since advised me), the far reaching effect it has had on my life will never truly end.

At the time of writing this book, I have no idea whether I have emerged from the Underworld or am still there. As I continue to slowly integrate myself back into society, I often feel a strong pull back to the shadows of the Underworld, as there is still much healing that needs to take place. At times I feel as if I am privy to my own private war and am now left picking over the pieces to see if there is anything salvageable from my previous existence. Having been faced with a life-threatening illness (the reoccurrence of which is never far from my mind), I was bluntly reminded of my own mortality and the importance of how I wish to spend the precious moments we call "life".

Someone once mentioned to me that my slow emergence was similar to that of a caterpillar on the verge of breaking out of its cocoon. Yet at times I feel that I have not allowed myself to integrate all the teachings I was expected to learn. This residual fear and uncertainty causes me to keep turning to look back to the comfort of the shadows of the Underworld as opposed to remaining focused on the unknown possibilities of what lies ahead of me. When I catch myself doing this I take a breath, for I know that with every step I take upwards I am not alone. The Dark Goddess is there guiding me, teaching me, assisting me in accepting and understanding my new identity. Her support enables me to stand strong in who I have become.

Nemesis by Soror Basilisk

# Continuing the Journey

SINCE 2006 I have been offering a workshop of the same name to people who wish to journey with different aspects of the Dark Goddess, 13 of which appear in this book. The timing of this workshop was usually held around the dark moon (the time of inwardness and contemplation) closest to 30 April, Samhain in the Southern Hemisphere, the Celtic festival of the dead. The time of the year when the veils between the land of the living and that of the Underworld were believed to be their thinnest.

Through the Temple of the Dark Moon, I offer both physical face to face workshops as well as online journeys for people wishing to enter into the Underworld realm of the Dark Goddess. The online journeys are designed to coincide with the thinning veil around Samhain, the Celtic festival of the dead. There are two auspicious times each year that this occurs. The Southern Veil journey commences just prior to the April full moon and runs until just prior to the May full moon, incorporating the timing of Samhain in the Southern Hemisphere, while the Northern Veil journey commences just prior to the October full moon and runs until just prior to the November full moon incorporating Samhain in the Northern Hemisphere. People will be able to participate in either online journey regardless of what hemisphere they reside in.

More information about these online journeys can be found through the Temple of the Dark Moon web page: www. templedarkmoon.com.

# About the Author

Frances Billinghurst has been a student of metaphysics, Goddess spirituality and the occult arts for most of her adult life. An initiate of a traditional style of contemporary witchcraft who founded the Temple of the Dark Moon in 1999, Frances is also a practicing occultist, a budding mythologist as well as an esoteric lecturer.

In 2003, Frances led the opening ritual of the New Zealand Pagan Fest with Chief Druid Philip Carr-Gomm, and in 2010, she was accompanied by occult philosopher Ramsay Dukes. She has also presented lectures at the Australian Wiccan Conference, the Australian Goddess Conference, worked with renowned Wiccan elders Janet Farrar and Gavin Bone, and held the position of secretary for the Pagan Alliance Incorporated (South Australia) for six consecutive years.

Aside from running an active coven, Frances is the author of *Dancing the Sacred Wheel: A Journey through the Southern Sabbats, In Her Sacred Name: Writings about the Divine Feminine* and *The Wytch's Circle*, as well as the editor of *Call of the God: An Anthology exploring the Divine Masculine within Modern Paganism*. Being a prolific writer Frances has had articles appear in numerous publications, including the Llewellyn *Witch's Calendar*, *The Cauldron* and *Circle*, as well as being a regular columnist for Australia's No.1 spiritual lifestyle magazine, *Insight*, for approximately 10 years. Her essays and poetry can further be found in anthologies including *Unto Herself: A Devotional Anthology for Independent Goddess* (edited by Ashley Horne and Bibliotheca Alexandrina), *A Mantle of Stars: A Devotional Anthology to the Queen of Heaven* (edited by Jen Connelly and Bibliotheca Alexandrina), *The Faerie Queens* (edited by Sorita d'Este and David Rankine), *Queen of Olympos: A Devotional Anthology to Hera and Iuno* (edited by Lykeia and Bibliotheca

Alexandrina), and *Blood, Bone and Blade: A Tribute to the Morrigan* (edited by Nicole Ross and Bibliotheca Alexandrina).

When she is not attempting to turn her patch of parched Australian dirt into something that slightly resembles the Hanging Gardens of Babylon, Frances also crafts an assortment of beaded jewellery, crystal mala beads and devotional beads. These items, together with many of the recommended incenses and oils that are mentioned in this book, are available for purchase through LunaNoire Creations - https://www.etsy.com/au/shop/LunaNoireCreations.

# About the Artist

Artwork for *Encountering the Dark Goddess* is designed by Soror Basilisk. With over 35 years' experience with magic and mediumship, her personal connection to deity and spirit is the major influence in all of her artwork. Creating the pieces for this work was an opportunity to re-connect with old friends and get to know and understand new ones.

Soror Basilisk has contributed articles and artwork to *Hekate Her Sacred Fires* (Avalonia), *The Cauldron* magazine, *Goddess of Sitra Ahra* (Black Tower Publishing), *Tricksters and Adversaries of the Left Hand Path* (Black Tower Publishing) and has exhibited artwork in the Adelaide Fringe Festival as part of the Cut Snake Collective.

She resides in the southern Antipodes with her partner of 25 years. She can be contacted at her Facebook profile www.facebook.com/sororbasilisk.

# Endnotes

1.  Berry, Wendell, "To Know the Dark", *The Selected Poems of Wendell Berry* (Counterpoint, 1999)
2.  Sogyal Rinpoche (2015), "Rest in Natural Great Peace", retrieved from http://sogyalrinpoche.blogspot.com
3.  Billinghurst, Frances, *In Her Sacred Name: Writings on the Divine feminine* (TDM Publishing, 2015)
4.  Commencing about 2.6 million years ago with Homo sapiens arriving about 200,000 years ago.
5.  The Hohle phallus (found in Hohle Fels Cave near Ulm in the Swabian Jura in Germany) is among the oldest phallic representation discovered, and is believed to be some 28,000 years old.
6.  If "matriarchal" refers to the worship of the goddess, "matrifocal" relates to the practice where the focus on the worship is on the matriarch, the feminine, but not to the exclusion of the masculine, the god. As such, "matrifocal" seems to be a more appropriate term to use.
7.  Throughout this book the abbreviation BCE ("Before Common Era") is used instead of BC ("Before Christ") and CE ("Common Era") instead of AD ("Anno Domini").
8.  https://en.wikipedia.org/wiki/Archetype
9.  The Egyptian Nut is not included in this book, however, my essay about her can be found in my earlier book, *In Her Sacred Name: Writings on the Divine Feminine* (TDM Publishing, 2015) as well as in *A Mantle of Stars: A Devotional for the Queen of Heaven*, Jen McConnel, editor (Bibliotheca Alexandrina, 2013)
10. Billinghurst, Frances, *In Her Sacred Name: Writings on the Divine Feminine* (TDM Publishing, 2015)
11. Chopra, Shambhari L, *Yogic Secrets of the Dark Goddess* (Wisdom Tree, 2008)

12. Harrison, Jane Ellen, *Prolegomena to the Study of Greek Religion* (Cambridge University Press, 1902)
13. Graves, Robert, *The White Goddess: A Historical Grammar of Poetic Myth* (Farrar, Straus & Gidux, 1961)
14. Mountainwater, Shekhinah, *Ariadne's Thread: A Workbook of Goddess Magic* (Crossing Press, 1991)
15. Orr, Emma Restall, *Kissing the Hag: The Dark Goddess and the Unacceptable Nature of Women*, (O Books, 2008)
16. ibid
17. ibid
18. Jung, Carl G, *On the Psychology of the Unconscious* (Dover Productions, 2003)
19. Jung, Carl G, *The Portable Jung* (Penguin, 1976)
20. Richo, David, *Shadow Dance: Liberating the Power and Creativity of Your Dark Side* (Shambhala Publications, 1999)
21. Wolkstein, Diane and Kramer, Samuel Noah, *Inanna: Queen of Heaven and Earth: Her Stories and Hymns from Sumer* (Harper Perennial, 1983)
22. ibid
23. ibid
24. ibid
25. ibid
26. Wilson, Robert Anton, *Ishtar Rising: Or, Why the Goddess Went to Hell and What to Expect Now That She's Returning* (New Falcon Publications, 1997)
27. Kűbler-Ross, Elizabeth, *On Death and Dying* (Simon & Schuster, 1997)
28. Chopra, Shambhari L, *Yogic Secrets of the Dark Goddess* (Wisdom Tree, 2008)
29. Opening lines from the ancient Babylonian text referred to as the *Enuma Elish*.
30. Mark, Joshua J, *Enuma Elish - The Babylonian Epic of Creation - Full Text*, retrieved from https://www.ancient.eu/article/225/enuma-elish---the-babylonian-epic-of-creation---fu

31. It is interesting to note that originally Tiamat was described as being devoted to her children, possibly indicating that the *Enuma Elish* we are familiar with today is possibly a compilation of various versions of this myth.

32. Mark, Joshua J, *Enuma Elish - The Babylonian Epic of Creation - Full Text*, retrieved from https://www.ancient.eu/article/225/enuma-elish---the-babylonian-epic-of-creation---fu/

33. Helle, Sophus Helle, "Tiamat (Goddess)", *Ancient Mesopotamian Gods and Goddesses* (Oracc and the UK Higher Education Academy, 2016), retrieved from http://oracc.museum.upenn.edu/amgg/listofdeities/tiamat

34. Wallis Budge, E.A., (trans), "Hymn to Sekhmet" from the *Egyptian Book of the Dead*

35. Approximately c.2,686 to 2,181 BCE when Egypt attained its first continuous peak of civilization.

36. Approximately from 1,550 to 1,069 BCE.

37. Amenhotep III was believed to have lived from 1,390 to 1,352 BCE

38. Author unknown

39. Patai, Raphael, *The Hebrew Goddess* (Wayne State University Press, 1978)

40. Believed to have been written by Jesus ben Sirach.

41. Zechariah 13:2, King James Bible

42. Patai, Raphael, *The Hebrew Goddess* (Wayne State University Press, 1978)

43. Hurwitz, Siegmund, *Lilith – The First Eve: Historical and Psychological Aspects of the Dark Feminine* (Daimon Verlag, 2008)

44. The "night hag syndrome" is so called where the victim awakes to find that he is being restrained and paralysed by an unseen force, which is now considered to be a "chemical malfunction" of the body.

45. Hurwitz, Siegmund, *Lilith – The First Eve: Historical and*

*Psychological Aspects of the Dark Feminine* (Daimon Verlag, 2008)

46. Langdon, Stephen Herbert, *The Mythology of All Races, Volume V: Semitic,* John Arnott MacCulloch (ed) (Cooper Square Publishers, Inc, 1964)

47. Hurwitz, Siegmund, *Lilith – The First Eve: Historical and Psychological Aspects of the Dark Feminine* (Daimon Verlag, 2008)

48. George, Demeter, *Mysteries of the Dark Moon: The Healing Power of the Dark Goddess* (HarperOne, 1992)

49. Ovid, "The Story of Medusa's Head", *The Metamorphoses,* retrieved from http://classics.mit.edu/Ovid/metam.4.fourth.html

50. Kottke, Amanda, 1998, *The Gorgons,* retrieved from https://web.archive.org/web/20100609204044/http://www.arthistory.sbc.edu/imageswomen/papers/kottkegorgon/gorgons.html

51. Evelyn-White, Hugh G., *Hesiod. The Homeric Hymns and Homerica with an English Translation* (Harvard University Press, 1914), retrieved from http://www.perseus.tufts.edu/hopper

52. Fraser, Sir James George, *Apollodorus: Library with an English Translation* (Harvard University Press, 1921), retrieved from http://www.perseus.tufts.edu/hopper

53. Gracia, Brittany, 2013, *Ancient History Encyclopaedia,* retrieved from https://www.ancient.eu/Medusa/

54. Monaghan, Patricia, *O, Mother Sun!: A New View of the Cosmic Feminine* (Crossing Press, 1994)

55. Shannon, Laura, *Medusa and Athena: Ancient Allies in Healing Women's Trauma,* retrieved from http://thegirlgod.blogspot.com.au/2017/06/medusa-and-athena-ancient-allies-in.html

56. Walters, Jamie, "She's Baaaaack (and a million times brighter)", retrieved from http://femininemojo.typepad.com/ssww/2007/11/shes-baaaaack-a.html

57. Graves, Robert, *The Greek Myths* (Penguin Classics, 2012)

58. The Gorgoneion masks are thought to have a common ancestor in the Mesopotamian head of Humbaba (a giant) mentioned in the *Epic of Gilgamesh* that dates back to the 3$^{rd}$ millennium BCE.

59. Kottke, Amanda, 1998, *The Gorgons*, retrieved from https://web.archive.org/web/20100609204044/http://www. arthistory.sbc.edu/imageswomen/papers/kottkegorgon/ gorgons.html

60. Shannon, Laura, "Medusa and Athena: Ancient Allies in Healing Women's Trauma" from *Revisioning Medusa: from Monster to Divine Wisdom* (Livingstone, G, Hendren, Tan Daley, P, editors, Girl God Publishing), retrieved from http://www.laurashannon.net/articles/105-2017-medusa-and-athena-ancient-allies-in-healing-women-s-trauma-in-g-livingstone-t-hendren-and-p-daley-eds-revisioning-medusa-from-monster-to-divine-wisdom-girl-god-publishing-206-222

61. An assortment of handcrafted specifically made prayer or worry beads together with crystal malas can be purchased online through LunaNoire Creations etsy store https:// www.etsy.com/au/shop/LunaNoireCreations

62. More ideas of using Franz Bardon's "Soul Mirror" exercise can be found at http://www.secrets-of-longevity-in-humans.com/positive-self-affirmations.html

63. Bradley, Marion Zimmer, The Mists of Avalon (Ballantine Books, 1987)

64. Malory, Sir Thomas, *Le Morte d'Arthur: King Arthur and of his Noble Knights of the Round Table* (Penguin Putnam Inc, 2010)

65. ibid

66. ibid

67. Sinclair-Wood, Lynne, *Creating Form from the Mist: Wisdom of Women in Celtic Myth and Mythology* (Capall Bann

Publishers, 2001)

68. Norako, Leila R. *Morgan le Fay*, retrieved from http://www. lin.rochester.edu/camelot/morgmenu.hmtl

69. Evans-Wentz, W.Y., *The Fairy-Faith in Celtic Countries* (Dover Publications, 2002

70. Matthews, John, *King Arthur: Dark Age Warrior and Mythic Hero* (Gramercy, 2004)

71. Bradley, Marion Zimmer, *The Mists of Avalon* (Ballantine Books, 1987)

72. ibid

73. Soul, Mary Lynn, *A Rebel and a Witch: The Historical and Ideological Function of Morgan Le Fay in Malory's Le Morte d'Arthur* (Ohio State University, 1994)

74. Black, Susa Morgan, *Morgan le Fay*, retrieved from http:// doirebhrighid.net/uploads/DB/pdf/articles/morgan.pdf

75. Jones, Kathy, *Priestess of Avalon, Priestess of the Goddess: A Renewed Spiritual Path for the 21st Century* (Green Magic, 2007)

76. ibid

77. Crowley, Aleister and Grant, Kenneth, "Kali" from *The Confessions of Aleister Crowley: An Autohagiography* (Penguin, 1995)

78. Chopra, Shambhari L, *Yogic Secrets of the Dark Goddess* (Wisdom Tree, 2008)

79. Depending on her aspect, while she is more commonly depicted has having four arms, Kali can be depicted as having up to 10 arms, the latter representing her as Mahakali (Mother Kali).

80. Woodroffe, John, *Hymns to the Goddess* (Library of Alexandria, 2015)

81. Avalon, Arthur, *Mahanirvana Tantra: Tantra of the Great Liberation* (Martino Fine Books, 2012)

82. Guin, Madhuri, "Kali the Goddess: Gentle Mother, Fierce Warrior", retrieved from http://www.dollsofindia.com/

library/kali/

83. The Kali Yuga is believed to last some 450,000 years, having commenced about 3,210 BCE.

84. The Kali Puja takes place during the "Festivals of Lights" that occurs around the night of the New Moon that occurs between mid-October and mid-November each year.

85. In a number of Eastern religions and philosophies the number 108 represents the universe. The individual numbers 1, 0, and 8 that make up 108 are said to represent one thing, nothing, and everything (infinity). 108 represents the ultimate reality of the universe as being simultaneously one, emptiness, and infinity. Interestingly, when the number of skulls that Kali wears around her waist are doubled, they equal 108.

86. Sowande, Fela and Ajanaku, Fagbemi, "Praises of Oya" from *Orúko Àmút òrunwá* (Oxford University Press, 1969)

87. Bascom, William, *Sixteen Cowries: Yoruba Divination from Africa to the New World* (Indiana University Press, 1980)

88. Beier, Ulla and Georgina, *Yoruba Myths* (Cambridge University Press, 1980)

89. BM Recordz, "Adebola", retrieved from http://www. aladeadebolayahoocom-adebola.blogspot.com/2013/07/ oriki-ifa.html

90. "Orphic Hymn to Hekate" trans. Hellenic Gods, retrieved from http://www.hellenicgods.org/the-orphic-hymn-to-hec ate-aekati---hekate

91. Johnston, Sarah Iles, *Hekate Soteira: A Study of Hekate's Roles in the Chaldean Oracles and Related Literature* (Scholars Press, 1990)

92. Hesiod, "Hymn to Hekate" from *Theogony*, retrieved from https://www.theoi.com/Text/HesiodTheogony.html

93. Hippolytus, *Philosophumena*, retrieved from https:// archive.org/stream/philosophumenaor01hippuoft/ philosophumenaor01hippuoft_djvu.txt

94. Long, A.P. (trans), "Orphic Hymn to Persephone", retrieved from http://www.asphodel-long.com/html/ orphic_hymn_ to_persephone.html

95. Spretnak, Charlene, *Lost Goddesses of Early Greece: A Collection of Pre-Hellenic Myths* (Beacon Press, 1992)

96. Jung, Carl, Kerényi, Karl, *Essays on the Science of Mythology: The Myth of the Divine Child and the Mysteries of Eleusis* (Princeton University Press, 1996)

97. Monaghan, Patricia, *The Goddess Path: Myths, Invocations, and Rituals* (Llewellyn Publications, 1999)

98. Foley, Helene P. Ed., *The Homeric Hymn to Demeter: Translation, Commentary, and Interpretive Essays* (Princeton University Press, 1994)

99. Spretnak, Charlene, *Lost Goddesses of Early Greece: A Collection of Pre-Hellenic Myths* (Beacon Press, 1992)

100. Foley, Helene P. Ed., *The Homeric Hymn to Demeter: Translation, Commentary, and Interpretive Essays* (Princeton University Press, 1994)

101. Spretnak, Charlene, *Lost Goddesses of Early Greece: A Collection of Pre-Hellenic Myths* (Beacon Press, 1992)

102. Downing, Christine, *The Goddess: Mythological Images of the Feminine* (Authors Choice Press, 2007)

103. Cott, Jonathon, *Isis and Osiris: Exploring the Goddess Myth* (Doubleday Dell Publishing Group, 1994)

104. Downing, Christine, *Psyche's Sisters: Reimaging the Meaning of Sisterhood* (HarperCollins, 1988)

105. Reed, Ellen Cannon, *Circle of Isis: Ancient Egyptian Magic for Modern Witches* (Career Press, 2008)

106. Levai, Jessica. "Nephthys and Seth: Anatomy of a Mythical Marriage" (paper presented at the 58th Annual Meeting of the American Research Center) http://citation.allacademic. com/meta/p_mla_apa_research_citation /1/7/6/8/9/ p176897_index.html

107. Downing, Christine, *Psyche's Sisters: Reimaging the Meaning*

*of Sisterhood* (HarperCollins, 1988)

108. ibid
109. Griffiths, J. Gywn (ed), *Plutarch's De Iside et Osiride* (University of Wales Press, 1970)
110. Butler, Edward, "Nephthys", retrieve from http://henadology.wordpress.com/theology/netjeru/nephthys
111. Wainwright, Gerald Avery, "Seshat and the Pharaoh", *Journal of Egyptian Archaeology*, Vol 26 (Feb 1941).
112. Jackson, Lesley, "Nephthys Silent Goddess of the Shadows", retrieved from http://www.Goddess-pages.co.uk/index.php /2011-issues/19-winter-2011/ item/510-nephthys-silent-Goddess-of-the-shadows
113. "Hymn to Nephthys" from Komir temple translated by Ian Ransom (2005), retrieved from http://z3.invisionfree.com / PACEdmonton /ar/t618.htm
114. Shafer, Byron Esely, and Arnold, Dieter, *Temples in Ancient Egypt* (Cornell University Press, 1997)
115. Budge, E.A. Wallis, *The Gods of Egypt* (Dover Publications, 1969)
116. Jackson, Lesley, "Nephthys: Silent Goddess of the Shadows", retrieved from (http://www.Goddess-pages.co.uk/index.php/2011-issues/19-winter-2011/item/510-nephthys-silent-Goddess-of-the-shadows)
117. Budge, E.A. Wallis, *The Gods of Egypt* (Dover Publications, 1969)
118. Mead, G R S, *Plutarch: Concerning The Mysteries of Isis and Osiris* (Kessinger Publishing, 2002)
119. Cintron, David A., *Aspects of Nephthys*, retrieved from www.cintronics.com/pdffiles/AspectsofNephthys
120. Forrest, M Isidora, retrieved from http://isiopolis.com/2012/03/10/isis-nephthys/
121. Temple Robert K, *The Sirius Mystery Excerpt* (1976), retrieved from http://www.bibliotecapleyades.net/universo/esp_sirio09.htm

122. Mercer, Samuel A.B. (trans.), *Pyramid Texts*, retrieved from http://www.sacred-texts.com/egy/pyt/index.htm
123. Metzer, Annedlinde, "Homage to Ereshkigal" (2009), retrieved from http://annelindesworld.blogspot.com/2012 /08/homage-to-ereshkigal.html
124. Eridu is an ancient Sumerian city believed to have been founded around 5,400 BCE
125. Enki as later referred to as Ea by the Babylonians
126. It was the Huluppu tree that the maid Lilith built her house and which Utu cut down in order to make Inanna a throne and bed (retrieved from http://www.piney.com/BaHulTree. html)
127. Other interpretations for Inanna's descent include that similar to Persephone, Inanna had heard the cries of the dead and therefore wanted to offer them her compassion. Alternatively, aside from being the Queen of Heaven and of the Earth, Inanna developed a desire to become the Queen of the Underworld as well by deposing Ereshkigal.
128. Wolkstein, Diana and Kramer, Samuel Noah, *Inanna: Queen of Heaven and Earth* (Harper & Row, 1983)
129. Lishtar, "Nergal and Ereshkigal: Re-Enchanting the Mesopotamian Underworld", retrieved from http://www. gatewaystobabylon.com/religion/nergalereshkigal2000. htm
130. An alternative version records Nergal taking Ereshkigal's throne by force.
131. Noble, Vicki Noble, *Shakti Woman: Feeling Our Fire, Healing Our World* (HarperSanFrancisco, 1991)
132. If you reside in the Northern Hemisphere then this path will wind to your left.
133. The opposite direction if you live in the Northern Hemisphere.
134. Guerber, H.A., "Loki's Offspring", *Myths of the Northern Lands*, retrieved from http://levigilant.com/Bulfinch_

Mythology/bulfinch.englishatheist.org/b/guerber/
Chapter19.htm

135. Sturluson, Snorri, *The Prose Edda: Gylfaginning*, retrieved from https://www.sacred-texts.com/neu/pre/ pre04.htm

136. Kvilhaug, Maria, *The Seed of Yggdrasil: Deciphering Hidden Messages in the Old Norse Myths* (Whyte Tracks, 2013)

137. Sturluson, Snorri, *The Prose Edda: Gylfaginning*, retrieved from https://www.sacred-texts.com/neu/pre/ pre04.htm

138. Faulkes, Anthony (trans.), *Edda* (Everyman, 1995)

139. ibid

140. ibid

141. ibid

142. Byock, Jesse (trans.), *The Prose Edda* (Penguin Classic, 2005)

143. ibid

144. Monaghan, Patricia, *The Goddess Companion: Daily Meditations on the Feminine Spirit* (Llewellyn Publications, 2000)

145. Wheeler, Post, "Vasilissa the Beautiful" *Russian Wonder Tales* (The Century Company, 1912). retrieved from http://www.surlalunefairytales.com/russian/russianwondertales/vasilissa.html

146. Natron is a chemical salt that was used in the preservation of mummies and can be made from baking a combination of salt and baking soda.

147. Traherne, Thomas, *Centuries of Meditations* (Cosimo Classics, 2007)

148. Goethe, Johann Wolfgang Von (trans. by Robert Bly), *The Holy Longing, in News of the Universe* (San Francisco: Sierra Club Books, 1980)

149. Harrison, Jane Ellen, *Prolegomena to the Study of Greek Religion* (Cambridge University Press, 1902)

150. Graves, Robert, *The White Goddess: A Historical Grammar of Poetic Myth* (Farrar, Straus & Gidux, 1961)

151. You can make your own anointing oil by adding a few drops

of essential oil into a carrier oil. I make and sell specific oil blends and other products for magical and ritual purposes through my esty store, LunaNoire Creations https://www.etsy.com/au/shop/LunaNoireCreations

152. WebMD, "Vitamins and Supplements: Pennyroyal", retrieved from https://www.webmd.com/vitamins/ai/ingredientmono-480/pennyroyal

153. Moon Giant, retrieved from https://www.moongiant.com/phase

154. Poppets can also be made from wax, wood, clay, plant roots and even paper.

155. For Northern Hemispheric readers draw an anti-clockwise spiral that has an arrow at the end.

156. Cain, Susan, *Quiet: The Power of Introverts in a World That Can't Stop Talking* (Broadway Books, 2013)

# Bibliography

The following books deal specifically with the Dark Goddess:

Beth, Rae, *Lamp of the Goddess: Lives and Teachings of a Priestess* (Samuel Weiser, 1994)

Bibliotheca Alexandrina, *Bearing Torches: A Devotional Anthology for Hekate* (Bibliotheca Alexandrina, 2009)

Chopra, Deepak, Williamson, Marianne and Ford, Debbie, *The Shadow Effect: Illuminating the Hidden Power of Your True Self* (HarperOne, 2011)

Clearly, Thomas and Aziz, Sartaz, *Twilight Goddess; Spiritual Feminism and Feminine Spirituality* (Shambhala, 2002)

Dawson, Tess, *Anointed: A Devotional Anthology for the Deities of the Near and Middle East* (Bibliotheca Alexandrina, 2011)

d'Este, Sorita, and Rankine, David, *Hekate Liminal Rites: A Study of the rituals, magic and symbols of the torch-bearing Triple Goddess of the Crossroads* (Avalonia, 2009)

De Luna, Inara and Lewis, H. Jeremiah, *Queen of the Great Below: An Anthology in Honor of Ereshkigal* (Bibliotheca Alexandrina, 2013)

George, Demeter, *Mysteries of the Dark Moon: The Healing Power of the Dark Goddess* (Harper Collins, 1992)

Gustafson, Fred (editor), *The Moonlit Path: Reflections on the Dark Feminine* (Nicholas Hays, 2003)

Horn, Ashley, *Unto Herself: A Devotional Anthology for Independent Goddesses* (Bibliotheca Alexandrina, 2012)

Krasskova, Galina, *Into the Great Below: A Devotional for Inanna and Ereshkigal* (Asphodel Press, 2010)

McLaren, Adam, *The Triple Goddess: An Exploration of the Archetypal Feminine* (Phanes Press, 1989)

Murdock, Maureen, *The Heroine's Journey: Woman's Quest for Wholeness* (Shambhala, 2013)

Perera, Sylvia Brinton, *Descent to the Goddess: A Way of Initiation for Women* (Inner City Books, 1984)

Roderick, Timothy, *Dark Moon Mysteries: Wisdom, Power and Magic of the Shadow World* (Llewellyn, 1996)

Spretnak, Charlene, *Lost Goddesses of Early Greece: A Collection of Pre-Hellenic Myths* (Beacon Press, 1992)

Starck, Marcia and Stein, Gynne, *The Dark Goddess: Dancing with the Shadow* (Crossing Press, 1993)

Wolkstein, Diane and Kramer, Samuel Noah, *Inanna: Queen of Heavens and Earth* (HarperCollins Publishers Inc., 1983)

Woodcroffe, Sir John, *Hymns to the Goddess and Hymn to Kali* (Ganesh & Co, 2001)

Woodman, Marion, *Dancing in the Flames: The Dark Goddess in the Transformation of Consciousness* (Shambhala, 1997)

# Index

**MOON
BOOKS**

## PAGANISM & SHAMANISM

What is Paganism? A religion, a spirituality, an alternative belief system, nature worship? You can find support for all these definitions (and many more) in dictionaries, encyclopaedias, and text books of religion, but subscribe to any one and the truth will evade you. Above all Paganism is a creative pursuit, an encounter with reality, an exploration of meaning and an expression of the soul. Druids, Heathens, Wiccans and others, all contribute their insights and literary riches to the Pagan tradition. Moon Books invites you to begin or to deepen your own encounter, right here, right now. If you have enjoyed this book, why not tell other readers by posting a review on your preferred book site.

# Recent bestsellers from Moon Books are:

## Journey to the Dark Goddess
How to Return to Your Soul
Jane Meredith
Discover the powerful secrets of the Dark Goddess and
transform your depression, grief and pain into healing
and integration.
Paperback: 978-1-84694-677-6 ebook: 978-1-78099-223-5

## Shamanic Reiki
Expanded Ways of Working with Universal Life Force Energy
Llyn Roberts, Robert Levy
Shamanism and Reiki are each powerful ways of healing; together,
their power multiplies. *Shamanic Reiki* introduces techniques to
help healers and Reiki practitioners tap ancient healing wisdom.
Paperback: 978-1-84694-037-8 ebook: 978-1-84694-650-9

## Pagan Portals – The Awen Alone
Walking the Path of the Solitary Druid
Joanna van der Hoeven
An introductory guide for the solitary Druid, *The Awen Alone* will
accompany you as you explore, and seek out your own place
within the natural world.
Paperback: 978-1-78279-547-6 ebook: 978-1-78279-546-9

## A Kitchen Witch's World of Magical Herbs & Plants
Rachel Patterson
A journey into the magical world of herbs and plants, filled with
magical uses, folklore, history and practical magic. By popular
writer, blogger and kitchen witch, Tansy Firedragon.
Paperback: 978-1-78279-621-3 ebook: 978-1-78279-620-6

**Medicine for the Soul**
The Complete Book of Shamanic Healing
Ross Heaven
All you will ever need to know about shamanic healing and how to
become your own shaman...
Paperback: 978-1-78099-419-2 ebook: 978-1-78099-420-8


**Shaman Pathways – The Druid Shaman**
Exploring the Celtic Otherworld
Danu Forest
A practical guide to Celtic shamanism with exercises and
techniques as well as traditional lore for exploring the Celtic
Otherworld.
Paperback: 978-1-78099-615-8 ebook: 978-1-78099-616-5


**Traditional Witchcraft for the Woods and Forests**
A Witch's Guide to the Woodland with Guided Meditations and
Pathworking
Mélusine Draco
A Witch's guide to walking alone in the woods, with guided
meditations and pathworking.
Paperback: 978-1-84694-803-9 ebook: 978-1-84694-804-6


**Naming the Goddess**
Trevor Greenfield
*Naming the Goddess* is written by over eighty adherents and
scholars of Goddess and Goddess Spirituality.
Paperback: 978-1-78279-476-9 ebook: 978-1-78279-475-2

**Shapeshifting into Higher Consciousness**
Heal and Transform Yourself and Our World with Ancient
Shamanic and Modern Methods
Llyn Roberts
Ancient and modern methods that you can use every day to
transform yourself and make a positive difference in the world.
Paperback: 978-1-84694-843-5 ebook: 978-1-84694-844-2

Readers of ebooks can buy or view any of these bestsellers by
clicking on the live link in the title. Most titles are published in
paperback and as an ebook. Paperbacks are available in traditional
bookshops. Both print and ebook formats are available online.

Find more titles and sign up to our readers' newsletter at
http://www.johnhuntpublishing.com/paganism
Follow us on Facebook at https://www.facebook.com/MoonBooks
and Twitter at https://twitter.com/MoonBooksJHP

# You might also like…

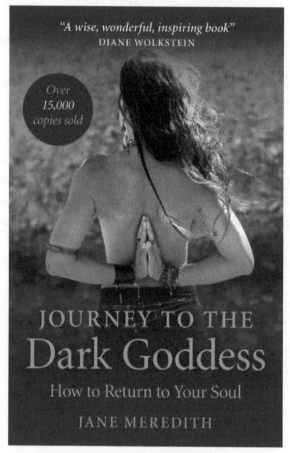

"A wise, wonderful, inspiring book"
DIANE WOLKSTEIN

Over 15,000 copies sold

JOURNEY TO THE
Dark Goddess
How to Return to Your Soul

JANE MEREDITH

## Journey to the Dark Goddess
### Jane Meredith

*Discover the powerful secrets of the Dark Goddess and transform your depression, grief and pain into healing and integration*

978-1-84694-677-6 (Paperback)
978-1-78099-223-5 (ebook)

You might also like...

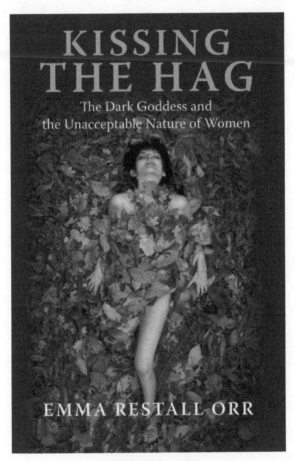

**Kissing the Hag**
Emma Restall Orr

*The Dark Goddess and the Unacceptable Nature of Women*

978-1-84694-157-3 (Paperback)
978-1-78099-970-8 (ebook)

You might also like…

**The Hidden Goddess**
Laurie Martin-Gardner

*The Quest for the Divine Feminine in the Judeo-Christian Tradition
- from Asherah to Mary Magdalene*

978-1-84694-157-3 (Paperback)
978-1-78099-970-8 (ebook)